Setting up in France

SETTING UP IN FRANCE

Laetitia De Warren
Catherine Nollet

MEREHURST PRESS
LONDON

Copyright © Laetitia De Warren 1988 and 1989

Published by
Merehurst Limited
Ferry House,
51–57 Lacy Road,
Putney, London
SW15 1PR

ISBN 1 85391 081 3
First edition published 1988
This edition published 1989
Reprinted 1989 (twice)

Typeset directly from computer disk by
Ponting–Green Publishing Services, London
Cover design by Ivor Claydon
Printed in Great Britain by Billings & Sons Ltd

CONTENTS

Laetitia de Warren is a French journalist. After an initial career in broadcasting – in particular as Foreign Affairs correspondent for French national radio – she married and settled in Britain. For ten years, she covered the British scene for various French national daily papers; she is now involved in launching a travel, arts and business magazine on France for the British public. Though based in France once again, she travels monthly between France and Britain. She had no trouble convincing her friend and country-woman Catherine Nollet to help her gather material for this book; as a French resident in Britain, Catherine was all too aware of the difficulties and problems encountered when settling on foreign soil and was more than ready to help others who may find themselves in a similar situation.

ACKNOWLEDGEMENTS

We would like to express our gratitude, for their advice and information, to:

Anne-Marie ACAT (Banque Transatlantique), Jacques BESSIERE (Alhérac International), François BOYER CHAMMARD (Cabinet Sarrut Le Poittevin Jalenques), Patrick GOYET and Pauline HALLAM (French Government Tourist Office), Michael FARRANT (French Associates), Bernadette ELFICK (A.P.E.L.), Katherine PAICE (*Farmers' Weekly*), Brigitte VANDENABEELE (Banque Transatlantique), as well as the French Consulate General in London, the French Industrial Development Board and the Centre for International Briefing.

Nord/
Pas-de-Calais

Picardy

Normandy

Paris
Ile de France

Lorraine Vosges

Champagne-
Ardenne

Alsace

Brittany

Western Loire

Val de Loire

Burgundy

Franche
Comté

Poitou-
Charentes

Limousin

Auvergne

Savoy

Dauphiny
Alpes

Rhône Valley

Aquitaine

Midi-Pyrénées

Languedoc-
Roussillon

Provence

Côte
d'Azur

Corsica

INTRODUCTION

A house in France...

The sun on the mimosas, the poppies in the wheatfields, the song of the cicadas, the chink of the pétanque balls, the daily 'apéritif' at the village café... A dream come true for thousands of Britons who, over the years, have acquired or built a property in their favourite part of France. But, like most dreams, it requires a lot of preliminary organizing, negotiating, coming and going and... counting all the available cash.

Buying a house in one's own country is a pretty traumatic experience; buying one in another country, where they speak another language, observe other laws and customs, have other priorities, other methods...and other plumbing systems, is definitely not a step to be taken lightly.

The object of this book is to offer the maximum amount of practical information on all the problems involved in buying, building or renting a house in France. This includes everything that is in any way connected with the operation itself, from obtaining a construction permit, through finding a builder, to putting your children into a French school.

We have also put together the various possibilities for short-term rental for those who just want to spend a holiday in France.

On the whole, the procedures for acquiring property are not so very different in France and in Britain – our legal, financial, fiscal and social systems are similar enough to have allowed the building of bridges between the two countries, thus making life a little bit easier for all of us. What we have tried to emphasise are those points so typical of French attitudes, laws and customs, that it would be difficult, if not downright dangerous, for a foreigner to ignore them. Forewarned is forearmed – so we hope that this book will provide you with sufficient ammunition to storm the citadel of French rules and regulations and come away with your little piece of Agincourt...somewhere under the luminous sky of France.

1
SETTING THE SCENE

When talking to British people who own property in France, one of the first things you notice is that they never say 'I have a house in France', but 'I have a house in Normandy/Provence/Dordogne' etc. And quite right too. If, in your mind's eye, you try to picture 'a house in France' without being more specific, you are not going to get a very clear image. The country is such a geographical, climatic, historic and architectural patchwork that styles vary not only from region to region, but sometimes from village to village. So there is no way you can avoid actually depositing that French house in a very precise spot.

Naturally France is not the only country that offers geographical variety; so do Britain, Italy or Spain, to name but a few in Europe. But the originality of France is that it combines variety with size – it is the largest country in Western Europe – and a central position on the European map which has played a vital role in shaping its history, its social evolution and, also, the style of its architecture.

When it comes to size, the figures speak for themselves:

total area of France: 543,965 sq. km
total area of Britain: 229,880 sq. km
total area of Spain (2nd largest country in Europe): 504,750 sq. km
total area of Sweden: 449,964 sq. km
total area of Italy: 301,268 sq. km
total area of West Germany: 248,687 sq. km

Positioned right in the middle of Western Europe, France has been visited, invaded or influenced by most of the peoples surrounding it. Quite a number of the French border regions actually belonged to the other countries at one time or another. All the efforts of the French monarchy and then the French republic to centralize and standardize the way the country works could never alter the fact

1

that a Basque north of the Pyrenees will always feel closer to a Basque south of the Pyrenees than to his countryman from Gascony; that Garibaldi, hero of the Italian *Risorgimento*, was born, the subject of an Italian king, in Nice, an Italian town until 1860; or that anyone born in Strasbourg in 1910 began life as a German citizen, went to school as a Frenchman, gave birth to German children during the Second World War and was finally allowed to settle down as a French national a mere 40 years ago. It is the same sun that beats down on the French and Italian Rivieras, the same snow that covers the rooftops on either side of the Rhine, the same rain that falls on Dunkirk and Ostend.

Anyone wishing to build an alpine chalet on the coast of Brittany would not only be considered a dangerous lunatic, but would be getting themselves into serious trouble with the authorities, because today builders must respect certain very specific architectural rules linked to the style traditionally used in the various parts of the country. This perennial duality between a very strong national identity and the pull of local roots that extend beyond administrative boundaries explains that mild schizophrenia inherent in the French character and way of life which an island-dweller must learn to take into account when juggling with the accumulated demands of central and local red tape.

PRICES

Notwithstanding these regional considerations, comparisons between prices and incomes when it comes to housing are only possible on a national scale. According to a survey carried out on behalf of the Nationwide Building Society (Nationwide Background Bulletin: "House Prices in Europe", Jan 1987), the average house prices for one-family homes were:

	Britain	*France*
in 1982	£25,550	£26,990
in 1984	£31,160	£29,820

The average annual change in house prices was:

	Britain		*France*
in 1982	+12		+5
in 1984	+9		+7

The number of manual working hours required to buy an average-priced house was:

	Britain		*France*
in 1982	8.750		10.434
in 1984	9.165		9.928

+4.7hrs   −4.8hrs

What all these figures boil down to, is that buying a house has lately become less expensive, on average, in France than in Britain. That, at least, seems to be the general trend, even though a Frenchman still has to work harder to buy a house that costs less. One of the main reasons is that mortgages – or loans, as they are known in France – are more difficult to obtain.

Britain actually has one of the highest rates of owner-occupation amongst Common Market countries. Only Ireland and Greece have higher. Owner-occupation in *Britain* is 62 per cent, while in *France* it is 51 per cent.

The difference, as you can see, is not as enormous as one might think, but it definitely exists. In general, the French real-estate system is much more geared to renting than its British counterpart, as the figures show: private rentals in *Britain* are 8 per cent, while in *France* they are 26 per cent.

Fewer mortgage facilities and more rental possibilities mean that most French people will not buy and sell their house every three or four years, as many British do not hesitate to do.

Unless they have the financial means to buy for investment, the French still tend to buy a house 'for the duration' and even for the sake of passing it on to their children. Often, therefore, they will buy a house, not where their job takes them (like the British), but where their roots are, where their parents come from or, failing that, where they would like to spend their retirement years. All this usually means a house in the country; until the last war, France was largely an agricultural nation so a Frenchman's grandparents, if not his parents, are liable to have been people of the land – farmers, smallholders ('peasants', as the British press likes to call them), squires, rich landowners, etc. It is quite common, therefore, for a Frenchman to buy a house in the country and rent his accommodation in town.

FLATS

French town-dwellers, you will notice, tend to live the life of a sandwich, with neighbours over and under, as opposed to their British counterparts, who still favour the lifestyle of the tinned sardine, with neighbours to left and right, even if it means having the bathroom in the basement and the bedroom in the attic.

There are all sorts of historical and sociological explanations for this, one of them being that in the mainly rural France of the nineteenth century, towns remained smaller and more compact than the sprawling conurbations brought about by the Industrial Revolution and the railways in Britain. There was, therefore, less room in French towns to build houses, let alone houses with gardens (except for the very rich) so blocks of flats were built instead.

In the last century, people of very different social conditions used to live in the same building – it was the floor you lived on that determined your social status. The ground floor would be given over to shops, with the owners or shopkeepers living over them on the first floor; that took care of 'trade'. The second floor was known as *l'étage noble*, the aristocratic floor – usually the one with the wider balconies, you will notice! That was for the *crème de la crème*, as the British would say. After that, the higher the floor, the lower the social status of the occupants, the reason being that, until the lift was invented, people had to use their feet and climb the stairs. On the very top floor, under the eaves, were the servants' quarters, the *chambres de bonnes*. Nowadays, the *chambres de bonnes* still belong to various flat-owners. So, if you rent a flat in an old building, you may find that you are also renting a *chambre de bonne* – very useful if you have to store a lot of suitcases! But sometimes the owner will have rented it separately to someone else – quite often a student, thus enabling French youth to pursue its quest for culture and higher education in living conditions that were rather gruesome even for a nineteenth-century skivvy!

Blocks of flats are not confined to towns or suburbs – you will find a great deal of them along the seafronts and in ski resorts (where municipalities have had to cope with the onrush of tourists) so even if your interest in French properties does not extend beyond the eventual acquisition of a holiday home, you may find that, in certain circumstances, buying a flat is an interesting option. It may even be the only option.

As most of these buildings are relatively new, it certainly eliminates the maintenance problems that arise from having to care for an individual house and garden from afar. Added to that is the question of cost: land can be exorbitantly expensive, especially along the Mediterranean coast so, unless you are prepared to go far inland, where the countryside is breathtaking but very hilly and dry, you may have no choice but to acquire a flat.

HOUSES

If you are going to settle in France for professional reasons and are therefore bringing your family, you may find that a house on the outskirts of a town can be an interesting proposition. It will, naturally be less expensive than a property in the town centre; furthermore, roads and motorways in France have developed in a way that makes suburban life and transport easy nowadays, to say nothing of French trains. Paris and its suburbs now have the very useful addition of the RER (*le Réseau Express Régional*), the fast and direct underground system independent from the Métro, that puts most of the surrounding localities within 15 minutes reach of the centre of the capital.

Some 20 or 25 years ago, many people bought or built houses in what was then the country, in areas that have since become the outskirts of the larger towns as urban development followed on the heels of the economic boom of the sixties and seventies. Now, quite a few of these people have reached retirement age and are selling their houses so that they can go and settle on their home ground or in the sun somewhere. If your life in Britain has (a) made you accustomed to living in a house and (b) turned you into a hardened commuter, you may prefer to give your family the benefit of a property with a garden for a price that will be more reasonable than for the same kind of house in the outskirts of London, or in the green belt.

If it is a holiday or retirement home in the country that you are looking for, then it is a question of combining climate, scenery, architecture and affordable price. The choice is very wide because – going back to France's recent history and social development – farms, whether large or small, were scattered all over the country and were being put to their original use until a generation or two ago. Then people had to leave the land to find work in towns and suburbs, so farms and villages were left for whoever was interested

Architectural Styles

The styles are varied, of course, but that variety is horizontal, rather than vertical; in other words, rural styles change from one place to another, but very little from one century to another. In France, the number of *communes* (towns, villages, hamlets, any group of houses and people) has hardly changed since the Middle Ages, compared to countries like Britain or Germany, where urban development has meant the end of a large number of the smaller communities. In proportion to the number of its inhabitants, France has actually three times more *communes* than any other country in the EEC. So when it comes to choice and variety, France certainly has a lot to offer.

Without going in detail into all the architectural styles and traditions throughout France – it would need hundreds of pages of explanations, illustrations and diagrams – we have tried to divide them roughly into some main categories, starting from the North.

The North and Pas de Calais

In the areas of Le Nord and Le Pas De Calais the houses are walled with pink brick, sometimes covered with a light-coloured white-wash. The roofs are often very steep and tiled with what are known as Flemish tiles. Their turned up edges are a reminder of the stepped gables on Belgian houses in Flanders. The houses themselves are solid, simple and rectangular; the woodwork is usually painted plain white, sometimes in bright colours.

Picardy

In Picardy the farm houses are long and low; the older ones have walls of clay or cob, the more recent are in brick, whitewashed or covered in white rendering. Elsewhere, the walls are of grey free-stone. To either side of the gabled roofs, the walls taper up towards the chimneys in a 'staircase' effect, called *échelles de moineaux* – 'sparrows ladders'. The 'sparrows' used to be the little chimney sweeps. In other areas, the roofs, covered in orange-coloured tiles called 'Northern pantiles' (*pannes du Nord*) come down very low at the back, nearly touching the ground. Some houses have their top floors covered in tiles to protect them against the wind. In this region, you also find some very beautiful fortified farms: the buildings are set out in a rectangle enclosing a courtyard where an ancient dovecote stands in solitary splendour.

Normandy

In Normandy half-timbered farms are often found in wooded areas. Where the houses have thatched roofs they inevitably resemble typical English cottages. In this area, famous for its cider and calvados, the various buildings which make up a farm are not attached to each other but scattered around a large orchard, called a *clos normand* (a Normandy enclosure). The house is constructed of a wooden framework filled either with daub or little tiles in a herringbone pattern.

In small market towns, the houses are often of brick; the windows and the edges of the walls may be trimmed with free-stone. The roofs are generally slate, in contrast to the half-timbered houses which, when they are not thatched, have orange-coloured tiles.

Ile de France

Although construction materials may vary a lot, what is character-istic about the houses in the Ile de France is the plaster rendering. This produces white walls topped with bluish slate roofs, or flat tiles where the colours go from grey to a reddish brown. On town houses (as on the old blocks of flats in Paris) the Mansard type of roof, with its elaborate skylights and small circular windows (*oeil de boeuf*), is typical of the region. The arched windowed doors have given rise to the expression 'French windows', also used by the French (*portes-fenêtres à la Française*).

Lorraine

In Lorraine houses are noted for their roofs, very broad and gently sloping, covered in grooved tiles (in the Metz region) or in slate (in the Vosges mountains). Another typical feature is the big arched carriage entrance; a whole area of the house in fact included barns and cellars, as working areas and living quarters were grouped under the same roof. The walls are usually of quarried limestone or sandstone, sometimes of granite nearer the Vosges. They are thick and squat, built to protect from the cold. The farmyards were often open spaces in front of the houses, which explains the wide streets of the villages in Lorraine. Today the compost heaps which stood on these areas have been replaced by flower-beds.

Alsace

In Alsace, half-timbered houses are to be found once again, but this style is very different from that of Normandy. They are much narrower and taller, often with several storeys; the round-tiled roofs are very steep and turned up at the edges, both to avoid snow piling up and to prevent it from falling too close to the walls. The chimneys of Alsacian houses are tall and thin and have been made famous by the storks which nest in them, in spring. These stork nests have gained a historic value: when Alsace was under German rule these migratory birds, able to come and go as they pleased, became a symbol of freedom.

Brittany, Vendée, Charentes

In Brittany the fishermens' houses resemble those on the Cornish coasts and in some corners of Wales. They are low and sturdy, with granite walls topped by slate roofs. They are built to provide

Alsace

Bretagne

protection against the wind and damp. The windows are small, usually opening towards the South.

Inland and in Vendée the houses are rendered with clay, roughcast with lime and often have roofs thatched with reeds from the surrounding marshes. The ridges of the roofs used to be decorated with a row of irises.

Rural houses in Brittany have only one floor, with a loft above running the length of the house; light is let into the loft by a sunken window in one of the upright gable ends or by skylights in the roof.

Farms in Charentes are very different – the influence of the South-West can be seen breaking through – with their two storeys, freestone walls and gently sloping roofs with grooved tiles.

Centre, Auvergne, Burgundy

Region of transition, of many different architectural styles, the Central region is often only thought of as the area that shelters the Loire châteaux. However, it is also thriving agricultural land, with many cattle markets and where the beef and cheese are well known for their quality. Rural life is simple. The farm is single-storeyed and consists of a single common room surrounded by cow-sheds, stables and even pigsties. Construction materials vary according to the soil. There are many freestone houses. On the banks of the Loire the most common material is porous limestone tuff, used in building many stately homes. It is a soft limestone, easily sculpted which explains why the façades of the houses are often decorated with moulding, inscriptions or statues. In the Loire Valley, slate, which is typical of the region, comes from the quarry of Trélazé which has produced most of the supply in France since the twelfth century.

The Auvergne is also an area of very varied architecture, to such an extent that it is difficult to find a specifically *auvergnat* house. Around Clermont-Ferrand the thatched houses are a reminder of the old sheep-folds called *burons*. Auvergne is a volcanic area, so lava, shale and Volvic stone are common building materials.

Burgundy is a rich area and its houses reflect this prosperity. Even the farms are often flanked by a tower. The roofs of the *Bourguignon* houses are very steeply pitched, and covered in varnished tiles decorated with geometrical designs. They are very famous, even if they can only be seen today on historical buildings like the *Hospices de Beaune*. In this wine-growing area, the cellar is an important place and often takes up the whole ground floor of the house. The living quarters are reached from outside by a monumental staircase. As for the walls, they are roughcast with stones set in round the windows and along the edges.

Perigord

Aquitaine: Pays Basque, Béarn, Périgord

These areas are well-liked by the British who have not forgotten the time when they were used to harvest grapes in Aquitaine. The styles are very varied. In the Landes the roofs have unequal slopes, one sometimes going right down to the ground. The house in the Landes gains in surface what it loses in height. Its wood timbered walls blend in with the surrounding forest.

The houses of Béarn, with walls of stones and pebbles set in mortar are covered by hipped slate roofs with edges that curve up slightly to keep the rain away from the walls.

In the Dordogne, tiles are generally used for the roofs, except in the region of Sarlat, where they are covered with slabs of stone, known as *lauzes*. In the south of the Dordogne, the red and rounded tiles are a symptom of the Mediterranean influence. Often, the roofs have triangular skylights called *outeaux* to ventilate the loft.

Dordogne

The colours of the stone used thoughout the Dordogne vary from white to grey to pale pink, according to the shade of the local sand. Like in many other French farmhouses, the first floor is used for living quarters, the ground floor for storing wine. There is often an outside stairway leading to a porticoed gallery. The tower attached to the end of the building is actually a dove-cote; its pointed roof rising above the rest of the building seems to turn the whole structure into a miniature *château*.

Languedoc

Toulouse is the area of pink brick: the traditional house is built lengthwise with living quarters, cellar and sheep-fold side by side. The roofs are in curved tiles, a style which continues down as far as the Mediterranean. Nearer the sea the white rendered houses are two-storeyed, with a wine cellar at ground level reached by a large carriage-type door framed in stone alongside the main entrance. The hay-loft is often just above the cellar, which leaves all the adjoining wing for living quarters.

Provence

Provence

The well-known farmhouse (*mas*) of Provence with its roof of curved tiles and its rendered walls in pink, ochre or sienna needs no introduction. However, this basic construction gives rise to a number of variations, sometimes within the same building complex. The *mas* was not originally a holiday house of course, but a farm where generations of farmers added, according to their needs, a barn here, a sheep-fold there, a dovecote, an external staircase and so on. The outside shutters are often painted in colours that recall those of surrounding nature: blues or greys, olive greens or warm and earthy browns. Sometimes the main building looks onto an interior courtyard, planted with cypress trees, illustrating the strong influence of neighbouring Italy. The houses of Provence have a double function: to protect against the very hot sun and against winds like the 'Mistral' which can blow very strongly indeed.

Savoie

The Alps

The alpine chalet is also familiar to most people, although this is
not the only style to be found in the mountains. Many mountain
homes are built not of wood but in rendered stone. The common
characteristic is the shape of the roof: slightly sloping, but
extending well beyond the sides of the house to protect them from
the snow and rain. In the past the ground floor used to be kept for
the cattle and the first floor for the farmers who, in winter, were
thus kept warm by the heat given off by the animals. The first floor
was reached by an external staircase leading on to a wooden
balcony that often continued all round the house.

USEFUL ADDRESSES

Association des Maisons
Paysannes de France
3 bis rue Léo Delibes
75016 Paris
Tel: 47 27 11 20
Tuesdays and Wednesdays
between 3 pm and 6 pm
Thursdays between 4 pm and
7 pm

Maison de la France
8 Avenue de l'Opéra
75001 Paris
Tel: 42 96 10 23

French Embassy – Cultural
Services
23 Cromwell Road
London SW7
Tel: 01-581 5292

Maisons des Provinces in Paris:

Alpes Dauphiné
2 Place André-Malraux
75001 Paris
Tel: 42 96 08 43/56

Alpes Savoie
16 Boulevard Haussmann
75009 Paris
Tel: 45 23 05 50

Alsace
39 Avenue des Champs Elysées
75008 Paris
Tel: 42 56 15 94

Auvergne
194 bis Rue de Rivoli
75001 Paris
Tel: 42 61 82 38

Aveyron
46 Rue Berger
75001 Paris
Tel: 42 36 84 63

Bretagne
Centre Commercial Maine
Montparnasse
17 Rue de l'Arrivée
75015 Paris
Tel: 45 38 73 15

Corse
12 Rue Godot de Mouroy
750092 Paris
Tel: 42 42 04 34

Franche-Comté
2 Boulevard de la Madeleine
75009 Paris
Tel: 42 66 26 28

Hautes Alpes
4 Avenue de l'Opéra
75001 Paris
Tel: 42 96 05 08

Lot-et-Garonne
15–17 Passage Choiseul
75002 Paris
Tel: 42 96 51 43

Nord Pas-de-Calais
18 Boulevard Haussmann
75009 Paris
Tel: 47 70 59 62

Poitou-Charentes
68 Rue du Cherche-Midi
75006 Paris
Tel: 42 22 83 74

Tarn
34 Avenue de Villiers
75017 Paris
Tel: 47 63 06 26

Drôme
14 Boulevard Haussmann
75009 Paris
Tel: 42 46 66 67

Gers et Armagnac
18 Boulevard Haussmann
75009 Paris
Tel: 47 70 39 61

Limousin
18 Boulevard Haussmann
75009 Paris
Tel: 47 70 32 63

Lozère
4 Rue Hautefeuille
75006 Paris
Tel: 43 54 26 64

Périgord
30 Rue Louis-Legrand
75002 Paris
Tel: 47 42 09 15

Pyrénées
15 Rue St-Augustin
75002 Paris
Tel: 42 61 58 18

2
BUYING FROM BRITAIN

Question: if I buy a house in France, does it mean that I will be rushing over there every other week to sort out dozens of practical problems?

Answer: not at all! Buying a property in France while living in Britain is not only possible but can be totally devoid of to-ings and fro-ings or any other complicated arrangements, for the simple reason that there are a certain number of British estate agents who can do most of the work for you.

You will find a list of names and addresses of relevant estate agents at the end of this chapter. Most of them also sell properties in the UK and elsewhere in Europe, so France is just part of their business.

There is actually only one agency that really specializes in properties in France, and that is French Associates in Robertsbridge, Sussex. French, by the way, happens to be the name of one of the founding partners and not the nationality of the company! People contact them from all over Britain, and with good reason. French Associates work hand-in-hand with a long list of estate agents throughout France; they have also, in the 15 years they have been in this business, acquired a thorough knowledge of the French conveyancing system and are perfectly able to do all the necessary paperwork, in both languages.

You will find in these next few pages a description of how things work if, say, you contact Michael Farrant, of French Associates.

If you phone in and express your interest in buying property in France, you will be sent a detailed information pack on how the real-estate system works in France, plus a standard list of houses and a questionnaire to fill in on the kind of property you require, its general location and the sort of price you are prepared to pay. Sometimes, the clients have a very precise idea of where they wish to live (because it is a favourite holiday location, or they have friends or relations there, etc); sometimes, they are very vague about the whole thing and only know that they would like to have a little holiday or retirement home in France, possibly somewhere sunny. If this is the case as far as you are concerned, the best thing is to go round to the agent for a chat; this will make it possible to pinpoint the type of area and property you could be interested in that would be in your price range.

Once this is done, it is advisable to try actually to go and explore the relevant areas, looking at the countryside, at the style of the houses, examining prices in the local estate agents' windows, etc. When you have decided on one or two areas, French Associates will give you a list of properties in those areas, as well as the names and addresses of their agents onthese agents
are highly qualified, quite a few speak fluent English, and most are members of the FNAIM – the National Federation of French Estate agents (for further details see Chapter 3).

You will soon find out that French estate agents do not have, as in Britain, very detailed descriptions of a property on their books; they prefer to take you out to have a look for yourself. In any case, French Associates will provide you with a letter of introduction in French for you to give to the agent on the spot; it outlines the kind of property you are looking for and the price you are willing to pay, so that, should you decide that the house you were originally interested in is not what you really want, the agent can suggest other possibilities; after all, the British agents' lists are not exhaustive, houses come and go and by the time you get to France there may be other properties just arrived on the market.

Once you have made a definite choice, one of two things can happen: (a) you can go back to Michael Farrant for the financial arrangements, or (b) you start off that side of things directly in France.

(a) You go back to Headquarters in Britain. You ask them to make an offer on your behalf. Once the actual price has been agreed upon, French Associates will get the local agent to send over the *Compromis de Vente*. This is a preliminary contract (details in Chapter 3) which will be checked over, mainly to make sure that there are no mistakes over addresses, dates of birth, etc. and that all legal formalities have been complied with. Then it will be sent to you for signing.

The *Compromis de Vente* must contain details of all rights to be enjoyed and restrictions affecting the property, including charges.

At this point, you will be required to pay a deposit on the purchase price – usually 10 per cent. This money will be deposited either with the notary (*notaire*) involved in the transaction or with the French estate agents if they have official authorization and proper guarantee. If the property is less than five years old, the deposit will be only 5 per cent. The contract is now binding on both parties.

(b) You have actually signed the *Compromis de Vente* while in France; you can then come back to your British agent for advice on how to proceed from there. To begin with, you do not need to contact a solicitor in Britain (because you are bound by contract), as the transactions are all handled in France by the notary. If, for various reasons, you do not wish to deal only with that particular notary, usually recommended by the agent, you are perfectly entitled to choose another as, after all, you will be the one paying the fees! Nevertheless, it is not always a very popular move because, if two notaries are involved, they will have to share the fee, which remains exactly the same. Should you be adamant, however, the local agent can give you the necessary address.

Once the deposit has been paid, French Associates arrange for copies of relevant documents to be sent to France pending the final act of sale. The local estate agents then tend to fade into the background and the British ones will be in direct contact with the notary. After a certain time – usually six to eight weeks – you will be asked for the balance of the purchase price plus the legal expenses, to be sent to the notary. Then will come the completion. If you cannot be present to sign the final act of sale, you will be requested to sign a power of attorney allowing one of the notary's clerks to sign on your behalf. In any case, before taking this final step, you can ask for a draft copy of the act of sale to make sure you really agree with everything stated there. Of course, it will be written in French...

When it comes to financing, most people tend to look for funds in Britain – which is the most logical thing to do. If you do not have the funds available from, say, an inheritance or the sale of a property, the simplest step is to remortgage your house. Not every British bank, building society or insurance company will do this if the second home is abroad, but your agent will obviously have a list of those who do. 'Legal and General' have a scheme whereby they will pay off your existing mortgage and give you a new mortgage including the sum needed for your purchase abroad. Up until now, no British company will accept the property abroad as a security. Nevertheless, this should be changing in a not-too-distant future, thanks to agreements that will eventually be reached between British and French financial organizations, whereby the French will be acting as guarantors for your property.

Transferring money to France is no problem, as there is no exchange control in Britain. For details on opening a bank account in France, see Chapter 5. There are, in any case, several ways of getting the money over.

(a) If you are already in France, and wish to pay the 10 per cent deposit so as to sign the *Compromis de Vente*, you can give a cheque in sterling to the French agent; it will be changed into Francs by the notary. It is preferable, though, to send the money from England through the banking system and ensure that the *Vente* contains a statement that the funds came from external sources so as to facilitate repatriation of funds on future sale.

(b) If you already had a purchase in mind before leaving Britain, you could instruct your British bank in advance to transfer the funds on the strength of a telephone call from you.

(c) If you are really in a hurry, the best way is to simply pop back to Britain and arrange for the transfer.

A word of warning: it is advisable, when you sign the *Compromis de Vente*, to be sure that you will be in a position to have the whole purchase sum available at the moment of signing the final act of sale. Otherwise, the sale may well fall through. At the most, the notary and vendor may agree to wait for a month or so, if you can prove that the money is forthcoming, but that is all. And don't forget: between the *Compromis* and the final act of sale, you may only have six to eight weeks' time.

Going through agents like French Associates will not cost you a penny more; they do not charge you anything because they share the existing commission with the French estate agent.

If, eventually, you wish to sell your house in France, there is nothing to stop you selling it directly to a purchaser in the UK. What you must take into account is the possibility of ups and downs in the exchange rate if the price of the property is advertised in France. Vendor and purchaser would be well advised to agree *in advance* on an exchange rate, and not to budge from that figure from beginning to end of the operation. The notary will be in charge of the proceedings, so the purchaser can have the money transferred to him first; or else, the money can be held in the UK by an independant party (eg a solicitor): once the sale is concluded, the relevant fees and expenses are sent to the notary and the rest of the money is transferred straight to the account of the vendor.

There is no exchange control in France at the moment but it could be reimposed; hence the need to record sources of funds. Before any funds can be exported from France it is nesessary to prove to the French Revenue that all taxes (including TVA) and debts have been paid. Normally a sum is retained by the Notaire.

Whether you are a resident of France or not, you as the vendor are liable for Capital Gains Tax if the property is not your main dwelling place. (For details on taxes, see Chapter 6.) If you are a non-resident, you must nominate a guarantor, to represent you vis à vis the French tax authorities for a span of four years. If you do not know anyone who will agree to do this, there are companies who will do it for a fee. If there is no question of tax liability, you can, with some success, request a dispensation (*une dispense*). The notary should be able to help you there.

Even if you have every intention of using the services of a British estate agent, it is important that you read Chapter 3: the more you know about the conveyancing system in France, the better you will be able to follow and control every stage of the operation.

BUYING A COMMERCIAL PROPERTY

Many peoples' dream of settling in France includes opening a small business somewhere in the sun – an antique shop, a wine bar, a restaurant, perhaps a hotel. There is, of course, absolutely nothing wrong with this idea, and many British nationals are today running successful businesses in France.

Nevertheless, before going into legal and practical details, it is vital to point out that there are some obvious, commonsense precautions to take if you do not want to end up with a commercial and financial disaster on your hands.

Take great care when buying a commercial property, especially if the proposed business involves importing products into France. Customs and tax problems can arise even if you appear to be following all the rules. Delays are unhelpful to your business even if they do not bankrupt you! This cautionary note particularly applies to buying in the South of France which may appear to be a law unto itself.

Going to France as a holidaymaker is very different from working there. You are launching yourself into a totally new ball game. You will be competing with people who are on their home ground, who know how to deal with their own countrymen and who also know their own laws and customs better than you do. Furthermore, the French, whatever their faults, are hardworking; so, unless you are prepared to work as hard as they do, and probably harder, you are not going to get very far.

If you intend to work in the same field as when you were in Britain, you have a better chance of succeeding. But, opening a wine bar if you were, say, a vicar or a telephone engineer, is going to put you on very sticky ground if you do not know exactly what you are doing. The British like to think that they are far better wine experts than the French (and in certain cases, so they are), but that does not mean the local people will necessarily appreciate being made to feel less knowledgeable than a foreigner, unless he manages to convince them of his prior experience and expertise. In France, food and drink are a major factor of national economy and are therefore in the hands of serious professionals – whether it is the market gardener, the grocer, the supermarket manager or the head of Moët et Chandon. The fat lady behind a flower stall in a colourful seaside market could probably write a book about growing lavender for the perfume industry and the young man serving at table in a provincial restaurant is probably the son, grandson and great-grandson of the present and previous owners and will follow in the footsteps of his forbears, bringing perhaps modern commercial and financial techniques to a solid, traditional business.

Those who do not have a family or personal experience are expected to have the necessary schooling. There are many very good schools, teaching cookery, catering or hotel management in France, with specializations in very precise branches. The same goes for wine.

It would therefore be a mistake to underestimate the training and experience of your eventual competitors.

Another mistake to avoid is falling in love with a location and deciding, against all odds, to set up a business there without being sure that such a business is actually needed in that particular spot. There are many instances of people opening hotels in beautiful country spots...where nobody ever goes because they are miles away from anything. This can only be possible if the hotel and restaurant are good enough to figure in well-known guides, and that kind of success is definitely not achieved overnight. So it means a lot of preliminary investment, unless your own family is prepared to get up at five o'clock every morning and work non-stop till around midnight.

If all these warnings have not put you off, if you have done your local market research to make sure your business will fulfill a demand and that you will be assured of regular supply, your next task will be to get a grasp of French commercial law, the tax system applied to business premises, the labour market, to name but a few of the subjects that will inevitably crop up. Entire volumes can be written – and have been written – on these and other relevant aspects of doing business in France and it is not the purpose of this book to go into all that.

What we will do, is advise you on whom to consult and what to read. While in Britain, you can start by contacting the British Overseas Trade Board, in particular its French Desk. They have lists of very useful addresses for people who want to start a business in France (some of which are given at the end of this chapter) such as British banks, bi-lingual lawyers, British chartered accountants, the relevant French government departments etc.

At the same time, contact the French Industrial Development Board in London, known in French as DATAR (*Délégation à l'Aménagement du Territoire et à l'Action Régionale*). Its main role is to encourage foreign business and investments in France. This includes letting you know about cash grants, tax incentives, subsidies for job training, etc. The DATAR publishes a series of booklets on doing business in France, French company law, the French tax system, industrial relations – all in English and all very clear and easy to read. These booklets will give you an important basic knowledge from which you can start building up your operation.

Either through a firm like French Associates or at a local estate agent in France, try and get hold of a periodical publication called *Partout*. It is published by a national network of estate agents called *Les Agences Françaises* and consists entirely of real-estate advertisements, with a large section dedicated to commercial and industrial premises. These are divided according to the nature of the business and not by geographical location. Going through this publication will give you an idea of the price range. You will notice a number of the advertisements come under the heading *Fonds de Commerce* and not *Magasins*. This means that you would be buying not the premises themselves but the business (*le fonds de commerce*), i.e., a certificate of goodwill. Sometimes, you can simply lease the business from the owner and become an independant manager (*gérant*); you will then operate the business as if it were your own and pay royalties to the owner. This happens quite often in the hotel, restaurant or caf trade.

When in France, and before coming to a definite conclusion, a good move is to contact the nearest Chamber of Commerce. Make an appointment with one of the people there and have a thorough discussion about the commercial possibilities of the town or village you are interested in. It is important to establish a good working relationship with the Chamber of Commerce because, once you have made up your mind, not only can they give you a good deal of advice and contacts, but they can also sort out a lot of red tape for you.

To begin with, as an EEC national, you are not required to have a commercial card or a work permit, but you must have a Resident's Permit. The Chamber of Commerce should be able to tell you whether it is in your interest to be self-employed (*travailleur indépendant*) or to form a company. The Chamber will also help you with all the forms that have to be filled in so that you can be registered at the *Registre du Commerce* and be given your personal registration number. The various Chambers of Commerce throughout France have launched what they call *Centres de Formalités pour Entreprises*: these centres will collect your inscription form plus a statement by the Town Hall (*Mairie*) of the locality you will be doing business in, confirming that the premises you will be working from are for commercial use. The centres will forward all this to the *Tribunal de Commerce* and, in due course, you will receive your registration number.

You will naturally have to pay taxes. What you pay will depend on whether you work as an individual or as a company. If you work as a self-employed trader in a small shop, the chances are that your personal and professional income will be considered as one and the same by the French tax authorities, whatever other sources of income you may have apart from your trade. Since 1987, if you form a limited company, losses can be deducted from the rest of your taxable income, under certain specific conditions. As a company, you will be required to pay corporate income tax. And, whether you form a company or not, you will have to pay a business licence tax.

And, of course, there is the inevitable VAT! The VAT system works more or less the same way in France as it does in Britain, with the proviso that in France the percentage is not the same for all goods and services (see Chapter 6). Nevertheless you need to know exactly how it works – all this is very clearly explained in the DATAR booklet *Summary of French Tax System*. In any case, the advice of a local accountant is invaluable; you would not run a business in Britain without one, so it stands to reason that you will need one in a country that is not your own.

If you intend to employ anyone, you will discover that workers in France are protected by a statutory labour code (*le Code du Travail*). This code, which has no counterpart in Britain, describes in great detail minimum conditions of employment, hours of work, holidays, health and safety measures, right to terminate contract, periods of notice, trade union rights, etc. There has been a statutory minimum wage in France since 1970; it is known as SMIC (*Salaire Minimum Interprofessionnel de Croissance*). As of July 1987, the SMIC was 4,704.96 Francs a month on a basis of a 39-hour working week.

Social Security charges are quite heavy and are mainly borne by the employer. They include supplementary pension, vocational training tax, transport tax (in large cities), apprenticeship tax, national housing fund, etc. All workers are entitled to five weeks' yearly holiday with full pay. The legal working week in France is 39 hours.

Buying a Farm

In the last few years, an increasing number of British farmers have been attracted to the idea of acquiring a farm in France. The reasons are obvious; there is more space, more choice and also the possibility of government grants. There are agents in Britain who cater for these prospective buyers. Nevertheless, the advice generally given is to start by doing your own shopping around in France. A good idea is to try and locate British farmers who are already settled in France and find out from them how they bought their property, what the problems are and how they are doing. The local British Consulate is the most obvious place to go – they will probably be able to put you on the track of one or two British farmers. Another solution is to contact *Farmers' Weekly magazine*. Not only do they know of British farmers in France and can put you in contact with them, but they themselves own a farm in Normandy, which you may be able to go and visit.

One of the most important things to remember, if you are intent on buying a farm in France, is that you will have to pay the total price of the property when signing the final act of sale, on a specific date. So, if you are counting on the sale of your own property in Britain to pay for the French farm, make sure that the sale has gone through and the money is available by the given date. It would also be a mistake to count on a possible grant for young farmers from the French government to complete the amount required for the sale. These grants can sometimes take quite a while to finalize and you may find the deal falling through because the money has not arrived on time.

Finally, the general consensus is that you will need a bi-lingual solicitor. You just cannot afford to see your personal and professional life ruined because of some legal clause you, or your solicitor, did not quite understand.

In short...

- Even if you are buying from Britain, it is advisable to explore the areas where you would like to have a property and get an idea of prices before contacting a British estate agent

- Financial arrangements can be made through the British estate agent or directly with their French counterpart

- Funds can be raised in Britain, generally by remortgaging your house

- Transferring money to France is no problem as there are no exchange controls but ensure the fact that money has come from external sources is recorded in the *Vente*.

- Be sure that you will have the purchase sum available in the six to eight weeks between signing the *Compromis de Vente* and the final act of sale

USEFUL ADDRESSES

UK Estate Agents Selling Properties in France

Alpine Apartment Agency
Hinton Manor
Eardisland Leominster
Herefordshire HR6 9BG
Tel: 05447 234

Properties in French Alps, Haute-Savoie ('Portes du Soleil', Chamonix, Annecy, Evian, Megeve, etc...)

Brian A. French & Associates
63 High Street
Robertsbridge
Sussex TN32 5AN
Tel: (0580) 880599

Catalan Properties Services
Well House Yard
Hare Street
Buntingford
Herts SG9 0EQ
Tel: 076389 224/511

Properties in Roussillon

Sarah Francis
1 Doneraile Street
Fulham
London SW6
Tel: 01-736 6855

Representing F.N.A.I.M
Agencies in Brittany and
Normandy

Francophiles Ltd
Barker Chambers
Barker Road
Maidstone
Kent ME16 8SF
Tel: 0622 688165

Properties in Normandy
(Deauville area)

John D. Wood
23 Berkeley Square
London W1X 6AL
Tel: 01-629 9050

Leisure Quest Estate
15 Saint-Thomas Street
Lymington
Hants SO41 9NB
Tel: 0590 79983

Properties and business in the
Languedoc Roussillon and South-
West areas of France

Residences Francaises
Saffron House
31 Clarence Street
Southend-on-Sea
Essex SS1 1BH
Tel: 0702 349898

Properties in the South of France
(Provence and Riviera) and also
most other parts of France

Ryder International
100a Ringwood Road
Walkford
Christchurch
Dorset BH23 5RF
Tel 04252 77178

Properties in Western France and
Languedoc area

Spratley & Co
33–34 Craven Street
London WC2N 5NP
Tel: 01-930 9803

Properties in Northern France
(Boulogne, Hardelot, Le
Touquet)

Les Traditionnelles Maisons
Francaises
Pantiles Chambers
85 High Street
Tunbridge Wells
Kent, TN1 1YG
Tel: 0892 48933

Properties in North-Western
France as well as Dordogne and
Riviera

Trou Normand
58 High Street
Shaftesbury
Dorset
Tel: (0747) 2841

Buying Commercial Property

Centre for International Briefing
The Castle
Farnham
Surrey GU9 OAG
Tel: (0252) 721194
Fax: 0252 721521

Department of Trade and
Industry
Exports to Europe Branch
1 Victoria Street
London SW1H OET
French Desk Tel: 01-215 5197

Farmers' Weekly journal
Carew House
Wallington
Surrey SM6 ODX
Tel: 01-661 4750

French Industrial Development
Board
21-24 Grosvenor Place
London SW1X 7HU
Tel: 01-235 5148
Tx: 28657

French Chamber of Commerce
Knightsbridge House
197 Knightsbridge
London SW7 1RZ
Tel: 01-225 5250
Tx: 269132 FRACOM LONDON

In France

British Embassy – Commercial
Department
35 Rue du Faubourg St Honoré
75008 Paris
Tel: 42 66 91 42
Tx: 2022-650264

Franco-British Chamber of
Commerce
8 Rue Cimaroas
75116 Paris
Tel: 45 05 13 08
Tx: 614806 BRCOMPA

Délégation à l'Aménagement du
Territoireet l'Action Régionale
(DATAR)
78 Avenue Marceau
75008 Paris
Tel: 47 20 07 90

Service du Registre du
Commerce
Avenue Paul Doumer
94110 ARCUEIL
Tel: 45 47 82 02

Business Consultants: Alhérac
International
26 Avenue Dode de la Brunerie
75016 Paris
Tel: 46 47 48 81

The French Federation of Estate
Agents
F.N.A.I.M
129 Rue du Faubourg Saint-
Honoré
F-75008 Paris
Tel: 42 25 24 26

3
ON THE SPOT PURCHASE

It may happen that while staying in or driving through a particular region of France, you come across a house that you fall in love with. The chances of seeing your dream-house on an estate agent's list in Britain are minimal, so you would do well to go through all the steps with the help of French-speaking people who are familiar with the system in France, but only make an on the spot purchase for small and simple transactions.

This system is not much more complex than in Great Britain but it is sufficiently different to give you the impression of having to start from scratch, even if you have already had experience of purchasing property in your own country. Unless you have a legal background yourself, speak fluent French and have a knowledge of the French legal system, it would be advisable to engage a French lawyer, or at least a spokesperson in whom you have complete confidence and who is capable of speaking English, to defend your interests.

THE LAWYER

It should be noted that the use of a lawyer in buying property is not a legal obligation as, in France, the legal individual involved in real-estate transactions is the notary (*le notaire*). However, as you will discover later, the notary who is involved in property transactions must remain completely neutral, not taking either party's side. In short, he is the referee, whereas the lawyer is on your side, paid by you to watch that you do not become totally lost in the linguistic maze of the French legal system, to help you understand and consent to each term of the contract that you have to sign and, in case of further litigation, to ensure that you have every means of defending yourself.

Moreover, if you spend the best part of your time in Britain, you can entrust him to take a certain number of steps on your behalf by giving him a limited power of attorney. He can also deal with representing your interests to the vendor or the estate agent up to the final signature of the contract, at which point the intervention of the notary will be necessary. He can, in particular, undertake bringing to a successful conclusion the offer of sale (*la promesse de vente*), the transfer of interests, and arbitrate in the sale, only leaving for the unquestionable competence of the notary the administrative and official formalities which arise.

Obviously the lawyer is worth his fee. It is up to you to decide if you want this expense. Don't forget that a lawyer is equally competent in fields other than real estate and you are going to have to familiarize yourself with certain other details that cannot be ignored, for example, your tax position in France, the laws governing legacies, the possibilities of transferring money etc.

How do you find a lawyer you can trust? There is nothing better, obviously, than personal recommendation, but more than that, the lawyer recommended by your French friends must be bi-lingual. The nearest British Consular representative provides a starting point for enquiries; in Paris the Council of Lawyers (*L'Ordre des Avocats*) is another source of information. It is obvious that the chances of finding a lawyer, or firm of lawyers with English links is greater in the Capital or main towns than in the depths of the countryside, but there is nothing to prevent a legal writer from Paris, Bordeaux, Lyon, Marseille or elsewhere defending your interests in any other part of France. The Franco-British Chamber of Commerce in Paris should also be in a position to give you the names of legal firms on its books.

It sometimes happens that a foreign client asks a lawyer to undertake personally the selection of properties within a limited area, in line with the criteria of style and price supplied to him, and the client only appears in person to make the final choice.

But if, as often happens, you prefer to operate on your own, that is where you will begin your long task of searching, visiting, and waiting, all complicated by the fact that you cannot dash over there every five minutes because you live abroad...

Do not let that prevent you from making the most of your stay in your favourite place and consulting the ads in the local press or in specialist magazines. This will soon give you an idea of current prices, of the type of property which matches your budget and of the estate agents likely to be selling what you require. Armed with this basic information you can then leave your address and telephone number with certain selected agents, providing them with as detailed as possible a list of your requirements so that they can contact you at home when an interesting bargain becomes available.

THE ESTATE AGENT

Your first professional contact in the whole operation will most probably be the estate agents. Their role is the same as that of their British counterparts, i.e. offering you properties, engaging in and following through negotiations and carrying the transaction through to its conclusion with the owner of the property. They must also keep an eye on the reliability of the transaction. In France the profession of estate agents is governed by laws, in particular the law of 21 January 1970 and the decree of 20 July 1972, which detail the conditions of application. Many estate agents are members of the FNAIM (National Federation of Estate Agents) the equivalent to the guilds of professional and skilled workers in Britain.

To be able to carry out his profession, an estate agent is constrained by law to display in his office the number of his professional charter, called 'The Charter of property and business transactions', renewable annually and signed by an official on behalf of the Prefect. He must also display the sum of his financial guarantee which allows him to receive monies from his clients. He must be guaranteed to the sum of at least 500,000 francs (about £50,000). If the total amount of the guarantee is less than this sum, the estate agent can in no way handle money on behalf of his client, apart from his own commission. In such cases notification of this restriction must be displayed in the office and you must only pay money (e.g. a deposit) to a man of law – a lawyer, notary or legal adviser – involved in the transaction.

If the estate agent does hold a guarantee he must display the name and address of the organization who are his guarantors, including the name of the bank and the account number which cover the guarantee.

On all correspondence, whether notepaper, documents or contracts, the estate agent must show the following:

- the number and place of issue of his professional charter
- the name and address of his business, including the nature of the business. The estate agent may also be a property manager, which gives him the right to collect rents, surety-bonds and expenses, on condition that he is in possession of a second professional charter – that of 'property administrator'
- the name and address of the organization which is his guarantor (for the agents who possess the financial guarantee).

It may happen that your first contact with an estate agent is made by telephone and that you only meet him face to face at the property he wants to show you round. As, in this case, you cannot examine the walls of his office to check that all the necessary documents are displayed, do not hesitate to ask him to show you his credentials if he does not automatically offer them. Don't be satisfied with his visiting card.

With regard to the way of doing business, the French estate agent is not very different from his British counterpart. It should be noted, however, that French law requires the agent to have a written order in his possession, signed by the owner of the house for sale or rent, authorizing him to carry out the transaction. It may be just a straightforward order (*mandat simple*). In this case the vendor reserves the right to negotiate directly with private individuals even if they have placed their business with one or several estate agents.

If it is an exclusive order (*mandat exclusif*), this means that the owner has placed the negotiations with a single agent, to the exclusion of all others. In this case the order must set out very clearly whether or not the owner reserves the right to negotiate with the eventual buyer or person renting.

These orders, which have time limits on them, must state the amount of the estate agent's fees, what they cover and who is liable to pay them. It is, therefore, very important to see this document.

In any case you must *never* part with money before signing a first written commitment to purchasing a property. This is also valid for rented property.

It must also be noted that the agent himself has legal protection. Once he has submitted to you a certain property from his lists, you cannot then short-circuit him and deal directly with the owner. Indeed, the agent is protected in this case by a penal clause which guarantees him payment of a sum equal to that of his commission.

ALTERNATIVES TO THE ESTATE AGENT

In France the estate agent is not the only professional allowed to sell property. It happens sometimes that an owner entrusts the sale of his house to a notary. The notary is under the same obligations as the estate agent. The characteristics of this situation are that one and the same person is in a position to handle the operation from start to finish because he holds the necessary powers to carry out all the legal matters pertaining to the transaction. But it must be emphasized, without questioning his integrity, that the notary undertakes the business at the request of one of the interested parties only; his client may be a local person with whom he is in the habit of doing business, whereas you are strangers who perhaps don't even speak the language. If, once you have acquired a property, you discover some points which you are not satisfied about, you risk bearing a grudge against the notary responsible for the transaction and thinking yourselves victims of some kind of local 'plot', which is not an ideal state of mind to be in when you are moving in among the locals in question. To avoid this kind of misunderstanding you could also engage a notary yourselves to represent you personally and to deal with the transactions at the same time as the vendor's notary. In this case the two notaries will share the fees between them according to the work done by each one. Each client undertakes to pay the part of the fee which falls due to his own notary.

Alternatively, you could engage a lawyer. In this case the fees are entirely your responsibility on top of other expenses. However, here you are assured of having someone to defend your case, whose role doesn't stop once the transaction is completed.

So now you are at a point where you have been sufficiently attracted by a property to consider entering into negotiations seriously. The estate agent will present you with a deed of contract; he must tell you in detail what this deed, that you are going to sign, contains.

BUYING A FINISHED HOUSE

If you are buying a house – new or old – which is already built and finished, you will sign an offer of sale (*une promesse de vente*).

The Unilateral Offer of Sale

The owner makes an offer of sale, on a specified dwelling, for a limited period of time which must be clearly stated. In exchange, he can ask that you pay a holding deposit (*une indemnité d'immobilisation*). On receiving this sum the proprietor must reserve his dwelling for you during the period covered by the offer of sale. He cannot therefore sell it to anyone else under the pretext that he has been offered a better price.

If you have decided to buy you are not obliged to wait until the end of the period specified in the offer of sale. You state your intention to buy, by lifting the option (*levant l'option*). The period of 'holding' is thus ended but this does not allow the owner to go and sell his house to anyone else or to take it off the market. If he backs out, for one reason or another, from selling you the property, you can sue him.

This offer of sale must be signed by you and by the owner and registered at the council offices (*la Mairie*) or the Prefecture (*la Préfecture*) within 10 days. The intervention of a notary is not necessary at this stage. It is what is called in France a 'simple contract' (*un acte sous seing privé*). At this point, bringing in a lawyer could be useful: he can have you sign the contract but without dating it. This could give you time, for example, to return to Britain to get the necessary money for the holding deposit and the document would only be dated at your signal. The period of reservation of the house only starts from that date, which leaves you more time to prepare for the next stages.

If you are quite sure of yourself and your financial situation you can sign a two-sided (bilateral) contract of sale (*promesse bi-latérale*).

The Bilateral Offer of Sale

In this type of agreement it is not only the owner who contracts to sell but you who contract to buy. This is called a synallagmatic contract – from the Greek word 'to unite'. Before signing, it is in your interest to check that the document contains all the necessary information, that the dwelling is really what you require and that you are in a position to finance the purchase.

However, it may happen for various reasons (e.g. administrative delays) that certain details are not provided at the time of signing. For your security, the law allows 'annulment' and 'suspension' clauses to be included. This means that, if at the moment of signing the actual contract of sale in front of the notary, the information which was not contained in the contract, but which was *due* to be provided has still not been provided, you are not held to the contract.

As a rule, the bilateral contract of sale includes the payment of a deposit of about 10 per cent of the overall price. If the stated conditions in the contract have not been fulfilled you will have your deposit refunded and the estate agent will not receive any fees.

The types of information which are accepted as 'suspensive conditions' and which must be given to you without question before you sign the final contract are in general:

- whether the vendor is really the owner of the property and whether he has the right to sell it to you
- whether the dwelling is mortgaged or not. If so, the sum of the mortgage must not exceed the sum of the sale as agreed
- whether the dwelling is the object of a seizure order which forbids the sale
- whether the various pre-emptive rights on the dwelling have been respected
- whether the dwelling is subject to any local regulations which are inconvenient or make the property unsuitable for your personal use

For your part, you must state if you have asked for a loan to buy the property, the amount, and conditions of of repayment. If you have not yet obtained the loan, or loans, you need, the contract of sale can only be finalized when you do; you will have the benefit of a determined period of time, a month at least. If at the end of this time, you have not obtained the loan, and if you can prove this, the contract will not take effect and the sums you have already paid should be reimbursed without any deduction or penalty, under the terms of the law of 13 July 1979 regarding the protection of borrowers. If you don't need to resort to borrowing, you should mention in the contract of sale that you are aware of the provisions of this law but are giving up your rights to invoke them.

NB: The contract should clearly state that if you back out of the purchase you lose your deposit but if the vendor backs out of the sale he must reimburse you *double* the amount deposited.

The Unilateral Offer of Purchase

In this case, it is you who make an offer to buy for a stated sum and within a stated period. This offer is usually accompanied by a deposit. This type of pre-contract only involves you, not the vendor, and does not guarantee that the property will be sold to you.

Do not forget, whatever the type of pre-contract you engage in, *never* pay money directly to the vendor but only to the estate agent, if he is entitled to receive it, or to the notary.

BUYING AN UNFINISHED HOUSE

You are buying a house which is in the process of being built. In this case, you will opt for a 'contract of reservation'.

This contract must compulsorily contain:

- a detailed description of the dwelling (area of living space, number of rooms etc.)
- the position of the dwelling, within the building if it is a flat, or on the plot if it is a detached house
- a list of communal services at your disposal
- the selling price of the dwelling and the possible reasons for a price rise (certain prices can in fact increase if the construction of the building lasts a year or more)
- the date on which the contract of sale will be signed
- the amount and conditions of the loans promised.

On signing this contract you will pay a deposit of guarantee:

5 per cent of the selling price if the contract is signed within a year

2 per cent of the selling price if the contract is signed within 1–2 years

No deposit of guarantee if the time period exceeds 2 years.

This deposit is placed in an escrow account in your name until the contract is signed.

By signing a contract of reservation you prove your willingness to buy, but certain conditions must be respected, otherwise the contract will be void.

The conditions of amendment are the following:

- the date of the contract of sale is not upheld
- the price of sale (leaving aside the increases stipulated at the start) is at least 5 per cent above the stated figure
- the sum of the loan promised to you is 10 per cent less than expected
- the dwelling described in the contract of sale does not match the description you were given in the contract of reservation
- one of the promised services has not been supplied
- you have not obtained the loan for which you applied, as precisely stated in the contract of reservation (still referring to the law of 13 July 1979).

In general, the estate agent must obtain a number of very detailed indications for you before you sign any kind of contract:

- the assurance that the vendor is really the owner of the dwelling
- an exact and detailed description of the property and its land boundaries
- the possible rights that may benefit another property owner (common walls, rights of ways etc.)
- the commitment of the owner to sell his property without mortgage or that the mortgage does not exceed the selling price
- the production of a certificate of town-planning specifying possible administrative rights (plans for compulsory purchase, inclusion in a protected area, bans on building etc) and services as foreseen in the short-term
- the amount of local tax payable for the previous year
- the insurance contract taken out on the building.

If all these points are not brought to your notice before the final signing of the contract it can lead to an annulment.

THE NOTARY

Whether negotiating the 'offer of sale' or the final contract, you will at some point find yourself before the notary if the matter is to be dealt with according to the rules of law.

The notary is an independent professional, but also a public officer appointed and controlled by the Ministry of Justice. His fundamental role is to give unquestionable authority and validity to all contracts. His authenticated deeds cannot be challenged – except if there has been an error or if negligence has been committed under his jurisdiction. Every deed concluded before the notary is an official commitment not only for you but also for your co-signatory; it can be set against a third party, even if this person was not involved at the start.

If you call in a notary at the moment of signing the 'offer of sale' this gives a solemn and official aspect to the deed which it will not have if signed only in front of the estate agent or lawyer. The notary is indeed capable of making this pre-contract an *acte notarié* (i.e. an act executed and authenticated by a notary) which gives it a considerable legal value in case of litigation. This provides extra security for you and likewise for the vendor, but means that you get involved from the beginning in the administrative process. It pertains to all the interested parties, therefore, to decide, depending on the circumstances, if it is in their interest to bring in a notary at this stage of the operation.

If you call in a notary for signing the offer of sale – or of purchase – he can help in several ways. For instance he may draw up the pre-contract without charge, and advise you on which suspension conditions to include. He will obtain the title-deeds of the property from the vendor, advise you on the merits of the selling price, the loans you are entitled to and obtain all the documentation you will need (rulings, certificates of conformity, insurance etc.). Finally he will advise you on all the fiscal aspects of the operation (local taxes, probable amounts of tax deduction etc.).

Next, the notary will witness the signing of the contract of purchase (this is where his intervention is compulsory), checking that all the conditions set out in the pre-contract have been fulfilled. After the signing, the notary will have the contract published at the estates index of the Office of Mortgages (*Bureau des*

Hypothèques). Indeed it is always necessary for the transfer of a property to be made official and available to anyone who may wish to know about it. The information supplied to the Office of Mortgages must be guaranteed by the signature of the notary. He will keep the original contract at his office where it can be inspected at any time.

To err is human and it may happen that the notary quite unwittingly supplies one or more incorrect items of information, or that one of his assistants makes a mistake. He must therefore, by law, sign a personal insurance covering his professional responsibility, which guarantees you against any error or mistake he may have made. Equally he must subscribe to a collective guarantee fund which covers in particular the amounts of money temporarily in his charge. When you open your account with the notary, he must give you a receipt. If the sum happened to disappear (theft, fire, or any kind of accident) you would be then assured of reimbursement. Remember that the responsibility of the notary is only binding if he has made a mistake or done something irregular that you are able to prove and which could be prejudicial to your case. If, after buying the property, you discover there is woodworm in the beams there is no point in blaming the notary.

How do you guard against this unfortunate type of surprise? In Britain the organization that gives you a property loan will automatically send a surveyor to check the state of the property. But, if your money comes from Britain, it is up to you to call in either an architect or a geometric expert (*géomètre-expert*). He will draw up a report which will allow you to make a knowledgeable decision, and if you think it necessary, he will try to get the selling price reduced. At this stage, the presence at your side of a lawyer, capable of telling you exactly how to act to obtain satisfaction, can prevent your getting involved in impossible litigation or giving up the property you want because you are not satisfied with its state of preservation and do not know how to go about making the vendor aware of these imperfections. There exist, as there does for lawyers, a Council of Architects (*Ordre des Architectes*) and one of Geometricians (*Ordre des Géomètres-experts*) who can provide you with a list of names for your area: by whatever means you employ one of these experts, check that he belongs to his professional order.

There are neither more nor less dishonest people in the real-estate business in France than anywhere else. However, as in all areas where there is a big demand, a foreigner is most vulnerable because he is less aware of the national laws – you must be careful not to fall into the hands of cowboys who will take advantage of your infatuation with the countryside and the mellow sky of France to swindle you. Don't forget these cowboys can be of any nationality... the temptation to throw yourself on the mercy of a fellow countryman is great and understandable but (and this advice comes directly from Britons living in France) be as vigilant about an Englishman as you would be with a Frenchman. Beware, in general, of anyone who says they can sort everything out by reducing the legal and administrative stages and proceedings so that you can have your property very quickly. The entire business of acquiring a house in France may seem complicated in comparison to what happens in Britain. If you take care to observe the normal procedure, however, you will be surrounded by guarantees and protections which are not always obtainable on the other side of the Channel. Though it seems to involve even more red-tape, the pre-contract avoids the infamous 'gazumping' which, in Britain, has reduced many a would-be purchaser to despondency.

APPOINTING A PROXY

But all this can mean that operations are spread out over several months, so you are not necessarily on the spot from beginning to end. You will have to give power of attorney to somebody. It is always possible to nominate some friend in whom you have complete confidence. It is also a good way of destroying a friendship. That is a statement arising from personal experience! Your proxy will spend sleepless nights wondering if he is really acting according to your wishes, needs, tastes etc. He will find he has a dreadful telephone bill from having called you every five minutes for confirmation of something; and at the slightest hint of difficulty, however good your intentions, you won't be able to stop yourself blaming him.

If you have a professional representative, a lawyer or judicial adviser, he should be able to save you the majority of day-to-day headaches (unless he doesn't know his job – it's up to you to draw your own conclusions). He can represent you at the moment of completion of the contract of sale which, in particular, can give rise to prolonged legal discussions which are difficult to follow for anyone not speaking perfect French. Your lawyer can prepare the deed of delegation for you and you can then sign it in the presence of a notary in France or at a French consulate back home.

The advantage of a legal adviser is even more obvious when it comes to unravelling the mysteries of taxation. He will be able to tell you, for instance, under what conditions you can benefit from tax reductions: the fact that you are a foreigner can sometimes, quite legally, allow you to buy under certain, more advantageous, tax conditions. However, as each case is considered individually it is up to your legal adviser to study with you the solutions which suit you best.

To get back to the 'cowboys', you can find yourself up against a vendor who is not bothered about getting involved in shady underhand deals (cash payments for example) to avoid the taxman. As you do not automatically know what should or should not be done, you risk running into trouble with the Treasury even before you have been able to move into your new property. If the Treasury should discover that there has been a direct exchange of money, you could end up paying a large fiscal "reassessment". This could happen to you even if you have committed no fraud whatsoever. For example, if you buy a house or land for a relatively modest price but the taxman knows that, in the near future, amenities will be provided (e.g. schools, sports stadiums, shops) which will increase the value, he can decide to tax you accordingly. A professional can help sort out many such problems in your best interest.

PERSONAL PRECAUTIONS TO BE TAKEN

Even before signing the pre-contract, you are strongly advised to take a number of personal precautions which will avoid subsequent problems:

- carefully examine, possibly with an expert (architect or geo-metrician), the state of the dwelling and check that it corresponds exactly to the description your estate agent has given you

- draw up – in the company of either the owner or the estate agent – an inventory, adding your own observations, particularly concerning essential services (water, electricity, heating)
- check up on the amount of local taxes either from the owner, the estate agent or the notary
- check the proximity and access to local services (schools, hospitals, shopping centres etc.). If you are buying a house for your retirement, a delightful little farm buried in the country is not necessarily the ideal thing. Remember that France is much bigger than Britain for the same number of inhabitants and distances are always much greater than they appear. Think about health and comfort and also, unfortunately, the problem of security for an isolated couple. These problems exist in France as they do elsewhere
- if the house in question is new or recently built ask if it has the label 'sound comfort' (*confort acoustique*) and if it is in the quality directory (*l'indicateur Qualitel*) which you can ask to inspect.

The Quality Directory

'Qualitel' is the name of an association created as a result of public pressure which issues a 'quality profile' of a house according to specifications put forward by the government and a number of building and housing specialists. It consists of standard criteria which determine the quality of the building and is necessary for all constructions of more than 100 properties for rent and 75 dwellings for sale.

The directory notes on a scale of 1–5 (from the worst to the best) objective elements that can be measured like noise, temperature, surface, wall linings, possibilities for installing domestic equipment, sanitation etc.

It is not interested in subjective elements, such as the architectural style nor does it judge the price of construction in relation to the quality of work.

ANIL

There exists in France an organization called 'The National Association for Information on Buildings' (ANIL). It has centres virtually everywhere across the country. Before engaging in the purchase, building, or renting of a house, you will find it invaluable to contact the nearest office (see addresses at the end of the book). You will find all the information, brochures and addresses concerning houses that you could need and it will prove to be of inestimable value. Even if this documentation is not in your native language you will no doubt find someone amongst your associates who will help you understand it. The information provided by ANIL is really worth the effort of getting over the language barrier.

SPECIAL ASPECTS OF PURCHASING

Co-ownership

This system is widespread in France. It consists in buying a flat in a block, and sharing the ownership of the whole building with purchasers of the other flats. It is what the Americans call a 'condominium'. Co-ownership can equally apply if you buy a detached house on a jointly-owned piece of land, though in this case the owners may choose a different system of administration (e.g. a housing association).

The flat is the property of the purchaser who is solely responsible for it. On the other hand, other parts of the building available for common use belong to all the owners; they are maintained and managed by the co-owners who make appropriate decisions by general vote. This concerns matters such as the roofing, walls, stairs, corridors and entrance.

Even though you are responsible for the use you put your own flat to, you are nevertheless required to be party to the terms of the co-ownership rules. These rules, for example, determine the amount you pay for heating, gas, maintenance etc. If business activity is not allowed in the building, you will not be able to turn your flat into a workshop, a photographic studio or offices. So it is in your interest to study the co-ownership rules right to the bottom line before buying your flat.

Not all co-owners necessarily have the same degree of responsibility, nor the same voting power in general meetings. The rights and duties of each owner depend on the value of their flat in relation to the others (price, size etc.). In short, the purchaser of a 5-roomed flat will have more responsibilities than the purchaser of a 1-roomed flat, but he will also have more power on the general committee.

To preside over the general committee and watch over the efficient daily running requires a trustee (syndic). This person is in charge of managing the building, making sure of the efficient running and maintenance and apportioning the charges. The owners can decide amongst themselves which one is to be trustee or apply to a company specializing in the management of buildings. This happens most often, in spite of the fact that a professional trustee must be paid, whereas a co-owner may do the job for nothing, only being reimbursed for his expenses (stationery, travelling, phone etc.). It is indeed difficult to ask a private individual, on top of his own job, to spend his evenings and weekends dealing with the building's business and then justify his actions to a group of individuals who, in all probability, will never agree between themselves or will gang up on him. Unless he is a saint it is difficult to imagine anyone accepting this kind of responsibility and criticism without eventually losing interest and being put off the job. It has to be said that co-ownership committees have now become part of French folklore. Stories of meetings turning into gang warfare are commonplace and the trustee needs to incorporate the qualities of orchestra conductor, snake charmer and lion-trainer if he is to survive.

The trustee is appointed for a maximum of three years by majority vote. He can be assisted by an advisory group whose members are chosen from among the co-owners. It is there to keep an eye on the administration and accounting of the trustee. In a block of flats where many people only come for the holidays (in the South of France for instance), it is not a bad idea to have an advisory group, however small, keeping an eye on the trustee.

Co-ownership charges

General charges cover all the maintenance problems of the block of flats. They are divided proportionally among the residents, and cover services, local taxes and the trustee's expenses.

Individual charges correspond to overall service payments: care-taking, upkeep of the garden, swimming pool and lift, refuse collection, etc. These are also divided according to their usefulness for the occupant. It is obvious that those in flats on the upper floors of the building have a greater need for lifts or stairs than those on the ground floor, so it is normal for those people to contribute more to their upkeep.

You must remember that your charges are not calculated according to the time you spend in your flat. Whether you spend a month in the summer or 365 days a year there, the charges are the same – they are based on theoretical, not actual use of the premises.

Annuity Purchase

Annuity purchase, known as *viager* (literally 'for life') is less widespread in France now than it used to be, but it does still exist, is perfectly legal and it may be in your interest to know of it, as someone may offer you this option, especially in country areas.

It consists in buying a property from an individual or perhaps an elderly couple, not with a lump sum but by regular instalments and letting them continue to use the house, or part of it, until their death. Under certain aspects, this may seem immoral, as the person acquiring the house is betting on the quick disappearance of the occupant – on the other hand it is a means for elderly people to have a comfortable income without having to leave their home or uproot themselves in order to survive.

The price obviously depends on the age of the vendor. It is calculated according to an average life expectancy of 70 for a man and 79 for a woman. The older the vendor, the higher the annuity. At the start, the purchaser hands over part of the price in cash (this is called the *bouquet*) which may be one quarter or one third of the total sum. The rest is divided into annual or monthly payments based on the age of the vendor. If, for example, he is a man of 60, the annuity would be repaid over 10 years or 120 months; for a woman of 50 it would be spread over 29 years or 328 months. If the vendor dies before the age limit, the purchaser will not have to pay the remaining sum.

The advantage of this system is that you can always pay the same sum as the years go by, whereas by paying on credit you know you will have to pay 25% more than the original price of the house. You do not have to take into account the fluctuations in interest rates, inflation or house prices.

Another element to be taken into account when calculating the price is the right of the vendor to continue living in part of the house. Sometimes the vendor does not want to stay there for personal reasons, but more frequently he reserves the right to keep a wing or a floor of the house, or even a corner of the garden to grow carrots and lettuces. In this case, of course, the rate of payment is lower than if the property had been completely empty.

In short...

- If you don't speak French fluently, you would be well advised to consult a bilingual solicitor who can ensure that the whole operation proceeds smoothly

- Ask the estate agent if he is a member of FNAIM (National Federation of Estate Agents)

- No payment must be made before a preliminary agreement has been signed; no money should be given directly to the vendor; it must go to the notary or, providing he is authorized to receive it, to the estate agent

- Ask who is going to be responsible for paying the agent's commission; this point must be clearly stated in the preliminary agreement

- You can, if you wish, have the preliminary agreement certified by a notary to avoid ulterior litigation. But you must be quite sure that you will not change your mind

- Do not hesitate to have the property surveyed before signing the contract, in case of structural problems

- In general, try to deal with experts belonging to a professional order or association

- If you are going to buy a flat, make sure that you know exactly what the annual expenses (*charges*) will be. They include: co-ownership expenses (local taxes, communal repairs and upkeep, fees for the administration, etc.) and collective expenses (garbage disposal, servicing of lifts, etc.). Expenses vary from one building to another, depending on location, social standing and other similar considerations.

François Boyer Chammard

Avocat à la Cour

Cabinet Sarrut Le Poittevin Jalenques

GENERAL LEGAL PRACTICE
CORPORATE LAW

47 Avenue Hoche   Tel: 47 63 45 63
75008 Paris   Tx: 642508 F

USEFUL ADDRESSES

Association Nationale pour
l'Information sur le Logement
(ANIL)
2 Boulevard St Martin
75010 Paris
Tel: 42 02 05 50

Confédération Nationale des
SyndicsdeCopropriété
53 Rue du Rocher
75008 Paris
Tel: 42 93 60 55

Ordre des Avocats à la Cour de
Paris
Palais de Justice
4 Boulevard du Palais
75001 Paris
Tel: 46 34 12 34

Chambre Interdépartementale des
Notaires
12 Avenue Victoria
75001 Paris
Tel: 42 33 71 06

Fédération Nationale des Agents
Immobiliers et Mandataires
(FNAIM)
129 Rue du Faubourg St Honoré
75008 Paris
Tel: 42 25 24 26
(Minitel: 3615 + FNAIM)

Groupement Syndical des
Copropriétaires
123 Rue St Lazare
75001 Paris
Tel: 43 87 56 65

Centre d'Etude du Viager
Grand Vabre
12320 Saint Cyprien sur
Dourdan

Bilingual Lawyer:
Me François Boyer Chammard
Cabinet Sarrut Le Poittevin
Jalenques
47 Avenue Hoche
75008 Paris
Tel: 47 63 45 63
Tx: 642508 F
Fax: (1)43 80 31 59

Qualitel (informations logements
neufs)
136 Boulevard St Germain
75006 Paris
Tel: 43 25 56 43

Centrale des Particuliers
(for person to person buying and
selling of property)
35 Avenue de Villiers
75017 Paris
Tel: 47 66 51 25
(Minitel: 3615 +
LANCENTRALE)

For general information on the legal fiscal on technical aspects
of buying, renovating or renting a property

Ministere de l'Equipement
244 Boulevard St Germain
75007 Paris
Tel: 45 44 39 93
(Minitel: 3615 + URBA)

or

23 Avenue Franklin Roosenvelt
75008 Paris
Tel: 42 56 45 86

4
BUILDING YOUR OWN HOUSE

Contrary to a number of neighbouring European countries – including Britain – France still has a lot of relatively open spaces. In view of this, there is a great deal of building activity both public and private, and when they can afford it the French tend to build their own houses.

It is advisable to use an independent French lawyer (not the Notaire) to oversee all stages of buying land and building on it. There are strict time limits to avoid having to pay tax or reimburse the vendor of the land; TVA is deferred on purchase of land provided the house is built within four years of the issue of the *Certificat d'Urbanisme*.

In the past, a rather lax building policy meant that everyone could give rein to their personal whims, which was often catastrophic from an aesthetic point of view. Today the guidelines are much stricter and builders must comply, even if only on a superficial level, with the different regional styles. The result has sometimes been a tendency towards uniformity in middle-range dwellings. But, on the whole, those who wish to build their own home benefit from a wide choice.

Starting by buying just a plot of land, rather than rushing into buying a house, can have its advantages, even if you live abroad. You do not have to start building straight away and you can simply put up a tent or park a caravan on it during your holidays. (After four years, from the date of the *certificat d'urbanisme* watch out for the land tax: it goes up in leaps and bounds on unbuilt land!) Alternatively, you could rent the land to a local farmer for grazing while you decide when and how you want to build. Whatever the case, there are several possibilities open to you: you can buy land from a private individual, either through a notary or an estate agent, or from local authorities which have a certain number of plots for sale.

The formalities governing the purchase of a plot are the same as for a house: unilateral or bilateral offer of sale or offer of purchase, as contained in the pre-contract and finalized subsequently by a contract signed in the presence of a notary. Once the plot has been chosen you can have a house built to your specifications, choosing your own architect and builder, or you can buy a house from a catalogue produced by a building group.

These last 20 years, the sale of building plots has been subject to very strict rules to avoid unrestricted building and, as far as possible, land and building speculation. Most land has been subject to building law since 1967: this law determines where and when land can be built on. As for the land which interests you, the relevant law is contained in a document which you have access to, called the 'Plan of Land Occupancy' (*Le Plan d'Occupation des Sols*). The plan is divided into development zones and your future plot will be situated in one of these zones. That is how you will find out if the public authorities have pre-emptive rights over your land or not: in certain zones, public authorities (municipal, local etc.) have the right to intervene and buy the land at a fixed sum even if private individuals are prepared to pay more. The idea is, precisely, to try to avoid uncontrolled price rises and speculation.

It is also interesting to know which zone your land is in, because the authorities may have already planned a number of communal services which will make it more valuable. If you are unaware that the land offered by Mr X will soon be close to a bus route or shopping centre you are going to wonder why it is more expensive than the land offered by Mr Y which has a better view...

If you want to look at the Plan of Land Occupancy you should go to the Departmental Office of Supply (*La Direction Départementale de l'Equipement*). As its name suggests, it has an office in each department. Another document which might be of interest to you is the Town Planning Charter (*Certificat d'Urbanisme*). This document can give more details than the estate agent or notary. It indicates two fundamental points:

- The planning dispositions (building density, size, appearance etc.) you must agree to before the land is allocated for building.

- The kind of building work allowed on the land.

The Charter also indicates the public services which are or will be installed nearby. To obtain this Charter you should go to the council offices of the district concerned, armed with a plan of your land. It may take up to two months before you receive a copy. It is therefore advisable to demand the Town-Planning Charter as a condition of purchase in the pre-contract.

PRECAUTIONS

The Plan of Land Occupancy and the Town Planning Charter are documents which can be indispensable if you want to know what dealings you are going to have with the local authorities. Even so, they cannot protect you against surprises due to possible misunderstandings of local ways, mentalities or even simply the geographical or geological situation of your land.

One point to resolve straightaway is the position of your land. If you intend spending your holidays on your proposed French property, you will obviously want to make the most of the light and sun. It is a question of making sure, once you have bought the land, that you have the house built facing the way you want.

If you are good at gardening, like so many British people, you should not find it too difficult to establish what the soil is like by looking at the kind of wild flowers growing there. It is important to ascertain the geological composition to avoid risks of flood and subsidence. No notary or Town Planning Charter will protect you from every eventuality and there is no point in taking it out on your neighbours if you have not taken the trouble from the start to do your own investigations.

Of course, the first precaution is to check very carefully the course of streams, rivers or lakes near to your land. Then inspect the vegetation carefully – if there are marsh plants growing there is a risk that the plot may flood. Do not hesitate to ask the locals and submit council employees to vigorous questioning. Finally, a little test which will have the added advantage of increasing your vocabulary: have someone show you on local maps, and if necessary translate, the names of hamlets, places, properties and even fields which surround your future land. If there is a reference to anything watery from fountains to reeds via ducks and frogs – there is a reason for it!

Do not forget, as well, that certain regions of France are

unfortunately prone to forest fire, especially in the south. That is the price France pays for being one of the most wooded countries in Europe. If you buy a piece of land which is very scrubby, remember that your first undertaking will be to clear it of everything that could start or spread a fire before you lay the first brick of your house.

You will ascertain from the composition of the ground if it is a reclaimed area. This will signify that part of the soil has come from excavations or from work elsewhere (roads, canals etc.) and it will never be as stable as the original land. Watch out for cracks later...

Another, more official step is to determine the 'viability' of the land. In other words, the possibility of having electricity, mains water and sewage installed; also are there roads, or just tracks leading to the plot? How will you have building materials delivered?

A fundamental aspect of buying a plot of land is the building regulations (*les servitudes*), that is the regulations imposed on a dwelling for the good either of the community or of private individuals, especially neighbours.

The Town-Planning Charter will tell you for example, if there are any administrative building regulations requiring you to build in a certain style or within certain height limits if it is a protected site or listed by the 'fine arts' (*les Beaux-Arts*) council. It will tell you if you are forbidden to plant trees or shrubs that might deprive your neighbours of light or obstruct electricity cables etc.

On the other hand, the Town-Planning Charter does not take into account private restrictions. You or your lawyer will have to go to the council offices or to the notary. There are a certain number of regulations regarding neighbouring properties or 'common ownership' (*mitoyenneté*) which can vary from area to area and mainly apply to the fences separating the plots. The rights, obligations and restrictions depend on who paid for the fence in the first place. The rights and restrictions concerning the height of the house (so it doesn't block the neighbours' light) and the way windows and balconies are facing must also be checked.

Municipal and public restrictions usually include:

- Right of way: obviously you may not want the whole village traipsing through your garden on Sundays on their way to church

- Water flow: if a water pipe crosses your land you cannot take it away or stop your neighbour connecting his own pipe to it.

If you build a garden or house wall right on the edge of your property you must make sure that the rainwater coming off the roof or timbers runs onto your land, not onto your neighbour's property or into the street.

Finally, remember that for generations, and still today, the most popular pastime in the French country areas is to drag one's neighbour to court at the slightest excuse, for instance that the pasture of one encroaches ever so slightly on the other's cornfield. It may be funny when you read this in a book. It is much less funny when you find yourself implicated in a quarrel that drags on until your grandchildren have their own grandchildren because your fourth begonia from the left has been laid claim to by your neighbour.

The reason for these quarrels lies less with the bad temper attributed to the French than with the fact that traditionally the sale of land is made without any basic guarantee – particularly building land. There is even a 'non-guarantee' clause included in the contract which prevents you from taking action against the vendor if there are problems with party walls, with the nature of the soil, or with the alignment.

At the present moment there is only one way to avoid these types of problems: marking out the boundaries (*le bornage*). This involves the accurate marking of the boundaries of the plot by marker posts, followed up by an official record accepted and signed by you and your neighbours. To go through this procedure you need to call in an expert geometrician, to draw up plans and survey maps of the land in question. He or she specifically fixes the boundaries, studies the amenities, sorts out the charges due and confirms the value of the land. This person is also in a position to fulfil the role of surveyor when it is a case of reporting on a ready-built house.

The geometrician can save you many problems, by telling you exactly what you can and cannot do by law. In France, as elsewhere, there is a land occupancy factor. The height and surface of your house may be limited according to the size of your plot, proximity of neighbours or the presence of a classified site or building etc.

PLANNING PERMISSION (Permis de Construire)

This is required if you are building a new house or even if you are adding to a building already in existence. You must supply:

- Details concerning your personal identity, the address of the plot, specifying whether you are already the owner or if it is under contract.
- A description including a plan of the plot.
- A plan of the building you wish to build with a description of its appearance, height, area, electrical and sanitary installations etc.
- A request for permission to demolish, if there are buildings you wish to get rid of.

Once completed, your file must be handed into the council offices and a receipt obtained or sent by registered post. You will receive a 'notice of receipt' (*avis de réception*) informing you that your file contains everything required. Permission is usually granted about two months after the notice of receipt was sent.

You can take charge of assembling the documents for building permission personally, otherwise your architect will deal with it. *In any case*, if your house is to have an overall surface area of more than 170sq. metres, you must employ an architect. The basic area (*hors oeuvre nette*) includes the entire floor area but does not include roof space, garages, terraces, attics, porches or courtyards. If you build a house of two or more storeys you have to add the area of each storey.

It is when you get building permission that you discover just how far you can go with your own tastes and personal desires. In particular, you have to build in a manner that will blend in with the region or even the district you want to live in. That means you will have to use certain building materials, certain coatings, and even, in some cases, certain colours in preference to others. This may seem to restrict personal liberties but these rules are the required minimum for protecting the beauty and harmony of the country-side.

In each French region, the Departmental Office of Supply (*Direction Départementale de l'Equipement*) will give you a free architectural service. They will help you in particular to respect local styles and keep you from making mistakes which might delay or cause rejection of your building permission.

Anyway, it's only a framework; within it, you can let your imagination roam free. The ruling is more or less strict depending on whether or not it concerns a classified site. It is always best not to follow your own whims, sidestepping permission, particularly in the case of restoration or renovation – even if some locals do it. A mayor who is a bit too indulgent or inclined to turn a blind eye can easily be replaced at the next election and an accommodating neighbour can sell up to more niggly newcomers who will not hesitate to alert the regional authorities; you then run the risk of having to demolish all you have built.

STARTING WORK

The Architect's Role

If you have decided to build your house to your own personal taste and if it is bigger than the famous 170sq.metres 'overall' area (which is not much, spread over several floors), you will need to hire an architect. He will help you define your plans according to your means and will draw up a definite pre-plan. If you agree with this, or once any modifications you require have been added, the architect will submit the building permission form in your name.

When you receive permission, the architect will help you to choose your builders and advise you on the estimates you have received. For people living abroad, or those not familiar with the system, the architect plays an essential role, from drawing up the design to overseeing the building work. He will keep you informed on work progress and alert you to any possible faults or building defects in the case of renovation.

To find an architect you can get information from the Departmental Office of Supply or the council offices, who will supply you with a list of professionals operating in your area.

Hiring Builders

Whether or not you have an architect, you are going to have to sign a contract with builders. The contents of this contract will depend on the negotiations you have had with the builders concerned. You must examine all the attendant conditions very carefully and make sure the following are included:

- A detailed estimate attached to the contract.
- A firm price, which can be fixed or subject to revision, depending on what has been decided at the time the contract is signed.
- An exact scale of payments.

This type of contract provides guarantees for the purchaser: 5% of the total price can be held back if the work is badly carried out, until an agreement is reached. If the builders are behind schedule there can be financial penalties.

As far as possible have the insurance number and the name of the building firm's insurance company written into the contract. They must be insured for the work you have asked them to do. On your part, you must definitely take out 'a damage to works' (*dommage-ouvrage*) insurance policy, which covers risks pertaining to the construction and is valid for ten years after the work has been completed.

Using Builder-designed Plans

If you prefer leaving the responsibility and effort of the house-building to someone else, you can go and see a builder who will provide you with a range of prepared house plans. When you have chosen the one you want, the builder will undertake to carry out the work. He will then be responsible in case of faults or delays.

You will both sign 'a blue-print construction contract for a private house' (*contrat de construction de maison individuelle sur plan*). This contract must include:

- A complete description of the house, with drafts and building programme.
- The price (fixed or subject to revision).
- The means of payment, with precise scales and dates of instalments.
- The proposed delivery dates.
- The guarantees required by law, in particular reimbursement in case of building permission not being obtained.

This last clause is of particular importance when you are the owner of the land from the outset. The builders cannot be sure the house they have proposed to you will automatically suit the plot in question. If on the other hand, they are selling you the land at the same time as the house, it would be particularly absurd if they had not dealt with these kinds of problems from the beginning and had suggested houses which were not suitable.

Buying a Ready-built House

There is a third possibility, which is to choose a plot and a ready designed house provided by a property developer. For those of you who dream of a Périgord farmhouse or a Breton manor house, the idea of choosing a ready-built dwelling can seem appalling especially for your holidays. Nevertheless, there are many situations where it would be a mistake to dismiss this type of solution out of hand, particularly where holiday homes are concerned. Many French people (and foreigners) are attracted by the possibility of buying a small, modern flat by the sea or in a ski resort. This gives them the opportunity of relaxing, without spending half their time rebuilding old stone, especially in places where the sun and the temperature allow them to spend most of the time outside, going indoors only to eat and sleep. The same reasoning applies to a bungalow near the beach or in a golfing complex, or to a mountain chalet.

As for the private house, built to live in all year round, it can also have advantages. The plots offered by promoters are often on the outskirts of a town; houses situated in a semi-rural area, sufficiently near to the hospital or shopping centres yet benefitting from peaceful and green surroundings are appreciated by families with young children and retired people. The majority of French towns are not really big and their suburbs are practically part of the countryside.

For a long time the main argument against this type of 'prefabricated' house was that they lacked quality, strength or beauty. Today house-builders in France are subject to strict quality controls; in this area, as in many others, everything is worth the price you are prepared to pay for it. You may have more problems with damp, rot or woodworm in a neglected old house than in new ones offered by builders. It's not a case of choosing between old and new, but between quality and mediocrity, whatever the age or style of the dwelling.

Your criteria of choice will therefore be: environment, price, style and size of dwelling. You can consult the catalogues obtained from an estate agent or from one of the specialist magazines; you can also visit exhibition villages to see the show houses; finally, if you wish to buy a flat, you can choose from a plan.

A piece of advice: before signing anything, it would be wise to check out the housing concern with the local Chamber of Commerce. This will at least give you an idea of the financial viability of the firm; if it is declared bankrupt before your house is finished, you risk having to take a series of long and expensive legal steps to get back the money you have already paid. If you choose from a catalogue, you will be paying by instalments and will not know precisely what particular work you will be paying for. So, if there is a problem with one of the suppliers, you will have great difficulty finding out if your money has been used to pay him or not. Normally the default of a supplier is not your problem, it is up to the property firm to sort it out, but if there are disappointments and delays it is always irritating to have no means of control over the situation. Some pre-emptive checking and the presence at your side of your lawyer are always good precautions to take.

In general, try to work out the exact price of the house, by taking into account the extras you will end up paying. The prices of houses in catalogues do not include charges for connection of gas, water and electricity. Also the initial price is always based on a completely flat plot. If your plot has some uneven areas, the price will increase.

Finally, you must take into account the cost of the legal steps the property developer will take, on your behalf, vis-à-vis the notary, the Treasury etc. All in all, this type of purchase will save you many headaches, but nothing is free and obviously you will pay the price for peace of mind. The type of contract you will sign is called a 'contract of sale of a dwelling for construction' (*contrat de vente d'immeuble à construire*).

INSURANCE

Whatever means you have chosen for building your house, one of the first precautions you must take is to check that you are well insured.

If you are taking charge of the building yourself, with or without the help of an architect, it is up to you, as soon as you have bought your plot, to take out a policy insuring against damages (*assurance-dommages-ouvrage*). This is required by law. This also applies if you buy an old house to renovate, as it covers risks of malpractice for ten years following restoration or construction.

THE FINAL STEPS

When the work is finished you must send three copies of a 'statement of completion of work' (*déclaration d'achèvement des travaux*) to the mayor within ten days. The mayor will then proceed to control the work, on the basis of six points in particular: position of building, exterior aspect, size, intended purpose, nature and quality of access. He will then deliver a 'conformity certificate' (*certificat de conformité*).

At last ... the final stage: the acceptance of the work. It is you who will officially state that the work has been completed, that it conforms to the contract document and that it has been carried out satisfactorily. This operation is legally very important as it entails the transfer of responsibility from the builder or contractor to you, the owner. From the moment of acceptance you become liable for any accident or damage which is not attributable to construction faults.

The contractor (or builder) will advise you when the time is right to go ahead with the acceptance of works. It is up to you to call together on a particular day, all the professionals with whom you have been dealing. If they cannot all come, at least the most important must be present. You should be accompanied by one or more people whom you can trust. Together, you can proceed to complete the inventory. That means you all go round the site several times checking that it conforms to the plans (dimensions, position, orientation of the doors and windows etc.), also to the specification description (including colour of carpets and curtains), and finally that the fittings are in good order. Any anomaly or damage should be mentioned in the report of acceptance; if you wait until you have taken possession, it will be much more difficult to prove that it was not your fault. If certain items cannot be checked immediately (heating, for example, if there is no fuel in the oil tank), this will not prevent you from accepting the work but, once again, these details must be mentioned in the report.

To find out exactly what steps you have to take and the exact points you must check, obtain a 'Guide for the Acceptance of Work' (*Guide de la Réception des Travaux*) from L'ANIL. This is a very comprehensive little book, well set-out, full of illustrations and reproductions of documents, which you can use straightforwardly as a memory-jogger, or as a notebook, to mark off points, one by one, as you complete them.

In short...

When buying a plot of land:

- Ask to see the *Certificat d'Urbanisme*, to find out what you can and cannot do on your plot, and for calculating TVA tax.

- Find out in which zone your plot is situated

- Do a survey of the terrain to determine the nature of the soil, its natural environment and the possibilities of access for water pipes, electricity cables, etc.

- Find out if your plot is subject to public or private obligations, like rights of way, limitations on building height and so on

When building the house:

- A building permit is compulsory

- You will have to employ an architect if your house is to have a net surface of more than 170 square metres

- When employing a builder, ask what sort of insurance he has and make sure that the policy is mentioned in the contract

- You personally must take out an insurance called *Dommage-Ouvrage*, valid for a period of 10 years

- When working out the costs, don't forget to include the supplements, like taxes, telephone, gas and electricity connections, etc

- In your own interest, use a solicitor

USEFUL ADDRESSES

SOCOTEC (Sociét de Contrôle Technique)
33 Avenue du Maine
75015 Paris
Tel: 45 38 52 73

For Consulting on Technical Details When Having a House Built

Chambre Syndicale des Artisans
du Bâtiment de Paris
12 Rue Flatters
75005 Paris
Tel: 47 07 86 62
(For advice on how to find a
plumber; electrician, etc.)

Ordre des Géomètres-Experts
40 Avenue Hoche
75008 Paris
Tel: 45 63 24 26
(To find a surveyor)

Ordre des Architectes Conseil
National
7 Rue de Chaillot
75016 Paris
Tel: 47 23 81 84

Fédération Nationale des
Promoteurs-Constructeurs
106 Rue de l'Université
75007 Paris
Tel: 47 05 44 36
(Guild of builders and promoters)

Fédération Nationale du
Bâtiment
9 Rue La Pérouse
75016 Paris
Tel: 47 20 71 53

Union Nationale des
Constructeurs de Maisons
Individuelles
3 Avenue du Président-Wilson
75016 Paris
Tel: 47 20 82 08

5

ARRANGING YOUR FINANCES

As a foreigner wishing to buy or build a property in France you will automatically fall into one of the two following categories:

- **Resident** You have been living in France for more than two years. In this case you can benefit from most of the same financial arrangements as French people.
- **Non-resident** Your main home is in Britain or a country other than France, or you have been living in France for less than 2 years. In this case you are subject to different rules – this does not necessarily mean that your financial options are more limited.
- Please note that these two categories apply specifically to your financial status and to the question of exchange control but *not* to your tax situation; you become a resident for tax purposes if you have been living in France for more than 183 days, i.e. around six months.

Within these two main categories are different sub-divisions, depending on whether your income comes from abroad, whether you are a civil servant, whether you are employed by a French or foreign firm or whether you want to obtain a loan in France or Britain.

OPENING A BANK ACCOUNT

Whatever your place of residence, there is a step you would be well advised to take – opening a bank account in France. Even if all the money for buying the property is coming from Britain, you will have a number of bills to pay on the spot and you might have difficulty convincing your suppliers to accept credit cards issued in a foreign country. When it comes to waiting for international

65

money orders or transfer of funds from your English bank account to that of your supplier, that is the quickest way to cause nervous breakdowns for all concerned!

Non-Residents

If you continue to live in Britain you will be considered as holding the status of non-resident in France and you will be able to open a bank account for foreigners. It is called a N.R. account in foreign francs (N.R. means non-resident). This is a simple procedure – you have to give your name and address in Britain and proof of identity (preferably your passport). With which bank would it be best for you to open an account? In a large town you may be able to find a branch of one of the main British banks or at least a French one affiliated to one of these. In any case, you should not have any problems opening an account at any French bank whatsoever. It is, however, best to choose your bank after checking that it is in a position to offer you the services needed in your specific situation. For example, would they agree to lend you money for the purchase and restoration of your house and, if so, under what conditions? Will they be in a position to manage your affairs in your absence?

In France there is a banking organization whose main business it is to take care of the business of non-residents, be they expatriate French people or foreigners with financial interests in France. This is the Banque Transatlantique, which has an office in London and has for generations specialized in the administration of foreign accounts, both private and commercial. As it is well aware of the day-to-day problems to be solved from afar, the Banque Transatlantique takes care of all your transactions down to the most minor ones. It deals with banking your income, transferring money between one country and another, buying and selling currency. It can help you buy a house by putting you in touch with a trustworthy estate agent; help you if you need a loan; even arrange to meet a member of your family at the airport, find spare parts for your car or buy a birthday present on your behalf.

Loans

At the Banque Transatlantique in Paris, as in London, you can obtain the necessary information if you want to borrow money to buy a property in France. At the moment, a non-resident foreigner wanting a property loan from a French banking organization has to give a personal contribution of at least 20 per cent of the value of the property they want to buy. Not all banks are necessarily able to supply this kind of loan, hence the importance of placing your affairs with specialized banks. Even if you do not want to borrow money straightaway, you may after several years want to extend or improve your property or maybe convert it into a restaurant or guesthouse.

The loan you receive can be in French Francs, but the bank may also arrange for you to have it, if you so wish, in a foreign currency – Swiss Francs or Dollars and for British people, in Sterling. The current interest rate for loans in French Francs varies between 10 and 12 per cent. This does not mean however, that your own particular interest rate will vary: on the contrary, from the moment the loan is granted, the interest remains fixed at the rate agreed upon at that time. For a loan in a foreign currency, the rates are revised every six months – based on the Paris international banking rates of exchange. (PIBOR).

A non-resident account used to be subject to stringent rules limiting the number of French Francs you could put into it and controlling your means of access to the francs in question; now things have changed. The bank will of course explain in detail all the operations you are entitled to carry out but, as things stand, there are practically no more restrictions on a non-resident account.

As regards debiting your account, you can carry out a whole series of operations, like paying by cheque for purchases all over France, using a French credit card, carrying out transfers of money, buying currency or travellers' cheques. For instance, should you sell your property in France you will have no difficulty transferring the proceeds back to the UK (after capital gain tax has been paid to the French authorities).

One last point to note: the advantage of this type of account is that it is no more subject to exchange controls than you are. In other words, you can transfer large sums to Britain even at a time when an economic or political decision subjects residents and French citizens to exchange restrictions.

If you are a government employee (diplomat, overseas civil servant etc.) you can open a non-resident account in domestic francs (*francs intérieurs*). You will thus benefit from the normal conditions reserved for residents and French citizens.

NB: If you are buying an unfinished house and are signing a 'contract of reservation' (see p. 36), the bank may be able to offer you a 'staggered' loan: instead of lending you an initial lump sum, they will advance money by instalments, as and when you need it (for instance, 5 per cent of the total amount when you pay the deposit, then the 30 per cent demanded on signing the contract, 35 per cent when the house is waterproofed, etc.). A point worth considering when it comes to paying interest.

Residents

If you decide to make your French house your main residence and to live there most of the year, you can benefit from a wide range of loans available to the French citizen. Even so, here and there there are some differences.

Covenant loans (prêts conventionnés)

These loans are granted by organizations or banks having signed a 'Covenant' with the State and can cover up to 90 per cent of the sum required to buy your property. There are obviously some conditions. The first is that it must relate to your principal residence, (i.e. the house where you live at least eight months a year). In addition, this residence must conform to strict rules concerning size and price. The covenanted loan may be spread out over 10 to 20 years with fixed or sliding repayments. The rate of interest varies according to the current situation but cannot exceed a limit fixed every quarter by the financial authorities (in June 1988, the limit was 9.65% for a 15 year loan and 10% for a 20 year loan).

Additional property loans

These are granted by two organizations whose names prove their links with the agricultural world: the '*Crédit Foncier*' and the '*Crédit Agricole*'. In the past these organizations dealt principally with finance linked to farming but today anyone can apply. Besides, the Credit Agricole is one of the most widely established banking organizations throughout France, and many French people, no matter what their professional business, have obtained a loan from them to buy or renovate their houses in the country. In December 1988, the rate of interest was on a scale from 9.85% to 11%

according to the nature of the loan. Repayments can be scaled over 15, 18 or 20 years.

House saving loan (epagne-logement)

This is the most difficult loan for a foreigner to obtain as it is only granted from 18 months to five years after opening a house savings account in France. It could therefore only interest those long-term residents likely to have foreseen well in advance they were going to buy a house. That means they know about house buying in France and already have all the necessary documents available to them. Nevertheless, it is worth pointing out the existence of this type of loan as it is quite popular with the French. It is, despite major differences, the nearest to the British building society system, from the point of view of the average consumer. Its logo, a little squirrel, can be seen in almost all medium and large towns in France. The rate of interest is currently 6.32%.

The traditional real-estate loan

This is the easiest loan to obtain, particularly for the foreigner, mostly from banks. Its advantage is that it is universal and can apply to everyone and for all sorts of housing ventures, whether buying, building or restoring new or old houses.

INSURANCE

In the majority of cases, as in Britain, the loan you obtain will be subject to your taking out life insurance. The rate is 0.54 per cent of the loan (so for a loan at 10.5 per cent interest, you will be paying, with insurance, 11.04 per cent).

Since 1984, you can also take out unemployment insurance. In general, this is given to those who have long service with their company. As regards government employees, it is considered they don't need it as they have job security.

TAX ADVANTAGES

For loans taken out for building, buying or for extensive repairs to a house, you can deduct part of the interest (up to 15.000FF) from your income tax.

The purchase of a new flat includes new and specific tax measures as described in Chapter 6.

You can equally well benefit from a reduction in tax if you claim expenses for energy conservation (insulation, double glazing etc.).

CREDIT CARDS

Whether you are resident, non-resident or a government employee, you are subject to a common rule that gives you the right to pay for your purchases in France with an international credit card issued by your bank. However, when paying by a credit card issued in France, your account is directly debited for the total sum. You do not pay a monthly sum to a credit company who serves as your guarantor to the vendor (as in Britain and the USA). The outcome is therefore exactly the same as if you pay by cheque, except that sometimes the amount due takes a little longer to be debited.

Moreover, you do not have to present a cheque guarantee card when you pay by cheque. Should a shop assistant ask for proof of identity, a passport, even a foreign one, will do. Visa-Carte Bleue is useful, if you use it to pay for your travels, because you automatically obtain insurance cover for the whole time you are away, whatever means of transport you use. (Carte Bleue is used nationally whereas Visa is used abroad, you may need to make sure that you obtain both if you travel a lot). Another advantage of Visa/ Carte Bleue is that it is accepted by any bank in France, and can even be used at any automatic till.

COUNTING THE COST

The prices given here are only meant to be indicative. They are subject to changes brought about by government decisions or the variations of a free market. This is not a cumulative list. It is up to you to pick out the expenses relevant to your particular case.

The estate agent

Estate agents are paid a commission on the transaction, as they are in Britain: no transaction, no commission. The percentages listed here are no longer compulsory by law, but most commissions have remained according to what used to be the legal scale.

Purchase price (Francs)	Commission (%)
up to 50,000	8
50,000–100,000	7
100,000–150,000	6
150,000–350,000	5
350,000–700,000	4

Over and above 700,000 Francs, you must negotiate the commission directly with the agent.

The notary

The notary can ask for a deposit to cover the expenses for setting up your dossier. Once the sale is completed, you will be sent a bill including:

- the notary's fee
- various expenses (office seals, papers, etc.)
- taxes due to the state

The notary's fees are also apportioned to the price of the purchase.

Purchase price (Francs)	Fees (%)
up to 20,000	5
up to 40,000	3.5
up to 110,000	1.65
over 110,000	0.82

If the notary was also in charge of the sale, in lieu of an estate agent, he will also bill you for 'negotiation fees', calculated thus:

5% of the price up to 120,000 Francs (plus 18.6% VAT)
2% over and above that sum, (plus 18.6% VAT).

Fees, taxes, commissions and legal expenses come to between 8 and 12 per cent of the price of the property.

Taxes

If you are buying a house that is not yet finished, *you* must pay VAT (18.6%). If the house was built less than five years before the sale, it is *the vendor* who pays the VAT and normally ask for an indemnity. Remember this if you are thinking of selling your seaside bungalow or apartment on the Riviera.

If the property is more than five years old, nobody pays VAT, but there are conveyancing taxes.

Here is a list of these taxes (in French):

> *Taxe d'enregistrement* (or *taxe de publicité foncière*): 2.60% of purchase price
> *Taxe départementale*: 1.60%
> *Taxe communale*: 1.20%
> *Taxe régionale*: around 1.60%; varies a little according to the region.

If you are building a house, you will not pay conveyancing taxes but will go back to paying good old VAT, at least on 70% of the cost of the land.

The surveyor (geomètre-expert)

Not compulsory but advisable if you are buying a house. Very useful if you are buying land.

His fees are normally determined by the length and difficulty of the work he will be doing for you. In any case, he must give you an estimate.

The architect

His fees are not subject to legal specifications. They will depend on the global cost of the operation, its difficulty and the exact role he will be playing in directing the work. To give you a general idea, his fees may amount to something between 8% and 12% (before tax) of the total cost of building. There are three ways in which you can pay him:

- You can give him a lump sum decided by mutual and pre-liminary agreement
- You can give him a commission based on the total cost of the building once the work is done (you will therefore not know how much you will be paying him until the whole operation is finished)
- You can pay him on an hourly basis (but this method should be limited to short-term operations; otherwise it can turn out to be rather expensive).

The builder and assorted specialists
Fees to be determined only on the basis of an estimate, followed by a signed contract. If any additional expenses appear along the way (as they inevitably do, whatever the country!), demand a new written estimate, to be signed by both parties.

It is obviously impossible to tell how much builders, plumbers, etc are going to cost you without knowing what sort of work is needed. Nevertheless, payments can be staggered in accordance with two possible scenarios:

(a) if the builder is guaranteed by a financial institution (ie. bank), it is known as *garantie extrinsèque* and payments can be staggered thus:

– 5% on signing the contract
– 10% on obtaining building permission
– 5% when the foundations have been dug
– 35% when the house is waterproof = 55% of total cost
– Another 40% when the various equipments have been installed
– Finally, the remaining 5% to be paid after official acceptance of the building by you, unless there is a dispute, in which case they are immobilized.

(b) If the builder is not guaranteed by a financial institution, it is known as *garantie intrinsèque*. The payments are then staggered differently:

– 3% on signing the contract
– Another 17% when the foundations have been dug
– Another 25% when the house is waterproof = 45% of total cost
– Another 40% when equipments have been installed
– Finally, the remaining 15% are paid, providing there is no problem, at official acceptance of the building.

Connections
Water – The cost depends on a series of factors such as the distance to the existing network, the nature of the soil to be dug up etc. You can count on a starting price of 5,000 Francs.
Electricity – Minimum price for an aerial connection: around 2,500 Francs. Around 3,000 Francs for an underground connection.

If it is simply a question of reactivating an existing connection, the price will be about 100 Francs.

Gas – Around 5,000 Francs for a new connection. Less than 200 Francs for a simple 'reconnection'.

Telephone – 250 Francs for installing a new line. Fifty Francs for reconnecting an existing one.

Insurance

If you are building your property you will need a building insurance (*assurance dommages-ouvrages*). It is compulsory.

Once the house is built, OR if you are buying an existing house OR if you are simply renting, you will have to take out a comprehensive insurance covering: fire-risk, theft, damages due to water, third party (for damages caused by members of your household). You may wish to take additional insurance to cover eventual damages occasioned by members of your family who are not permanent residents or by domestic animals or damages linked to the house (a tile falling from the roof, for instance), or to cover storm damage or natural disasters.

In short...

- First step: open a bank account, whether you are a permanent resident or a non-resident, preferably with a bank that is used to dealing with foreign transactions

- Remember that the use of an international credit card can make life easier for you

- If you are a resident in France, you can obtain a loan to buy or build a house provided you can offer the necessary financial and professional guarantees

- You will be asked to take out life insurance if you get a loan

USEFUL ADDRESSES

Banque Transatlantique –
London
103 Mount Street
London W1Y 5HE
Tel: 01-493 6717
Tx 269865
Fax: (1) 495 1018

Banque Transatlantique Paris
17 Boulevard Haussmann
75009 Paris
Tel: 40 22 80 00
Tx: 650729
Fax: (1) 48 24 01 75

Crédit Agricole Mutuel de L'Ile
de France
26 Quai de la Râpeé
75012 Paris
Tel: 43 46 22 22

Legal and General
Financial Consultancy Services
Middleton House
49 High Street
Horley
Surrey RH6 7BN
Tel: (0293) 785588

British Banks in Paris

Barclays Bank
33 Rue du Quatre Septembre
75002 Paris
Tel: 40 06 85 85

Westminster Bank (International)
18 Place Vendôme
75001 Paris
Tel: 42 60 37 40

Midland Bank
6 Rue Piccini
75016 Paris
Tel: 45 02 80 80

Lloyds Bank (France)
43 Boulevard des Capucines
75002 Paris
Tel: 40 15 33 33

6
FRENCH TAXES

What makes you, a foreigner, liable under the French tax system? How do you avoid finding yourself, unwittingly, in difficulties with the tax authorities in France or Britain? And finally, how do you avoid paying the same taxes twice?

These three fundamental questions give rise to answers of varying complexity. In general you need to know some of the main principles of the French tax system and make a point of clearly stating your own personal position to the proper authorities so that they come up with the information relating to your particular case.

Please note that a bi-lateral agreement on tax exists between France and Britain, designed to prevent you having to pay your taxes twice. However, you will find that this agreement will work better in your favour if you take the trouble to go, with your file, to your tax office in Britain or the tax inspector in the area of France where you have your property, and explain your situation. Should the need arise, your lawyer or French financial advisor can take these steps for you in France. Be cautious and methodical in this respect otherwise you may end up paying more tax than necessary.

WEALTH TAX

Wealth tax comes into effect in France on 1 January 1989 and is based on net assets. There is no relief for spouse or minor children as in income tax. The tax becomes payable at 4 million Fr (0.5%) and rises to 1.1%.

INCOME TAX

The French, like the British, are liable for income tax. If you go and settle full-time in France and request a residence permit, you can expect to have to pay income tax to the French. But take care: in order to claim what he considers you owe him, the taxman is not going to be satisfied with just knowing whether or not you have a long-stay visitor's permit. What he will want to know is your tax address (*domicile fiscal*).

To find out if this tax address is in France you need to know whether your situation corresponds to certain precise criteria:

- your *main residence* must be in France. That does not necessarily mean that you own a house in France, but that you live in the country more than 183 days in any tax year (which begins on 1 January). This still applies if your immediate family (spouse and children) are living in France for the same period, even if you personally are abroad on business.
- your *job* must be in France. Working for a foreign company does not exempt you from paying income tax even if your salary comes from abroad.

If you are not earning wages but your main source of income is in France, then your tax address is considered to be in France, even if you don't live in that country. If, say, you live off income from rented properties in France then that is where your tax address will be.

The fundamental outcome of having France as a tax address is that you have to declare *all* your income to the French taxman, wherever it comes from, even from the farthest corners of the planet. That is why you must definitely find out about any agreements between France and the country (or countries) from which you get your income. Please note that the Franco-British agreement does not include the Channel Islands, which are considered a 'tax-haven' and thus are not very popular with the French fiscal authorities.

The advice of a good lawyer or accountant will be *essential* because when it comes to deciding who gets your money, tax offices on both sides of the Channel can suddenly become very patriotic.

Calculating Your Tax

Your taxable income depends first and foremost on your family situation, as in Britain. Only your own adviser can help you to fill in your tax forms – especially if you have an income from abroad. It is therefore useless to go into complicated details – there would no doubt be as many exceptions to the rules as there are readers... But there are, even so, some fundamental differences between the French and English tax systems which everyone should know about.

Taxpayers in France pay taxes on their income for the *preceding* year, not the current one. In other words the tax paid, for instance, in 1987, is calculated on the income for 1986. It would be difficult to do otherwise as the tax return has to be filled in and submitted to the taxman in February, i.e. at the beginning of the year; it is hard to imagine how a taxpayer could know exactly what his or her income was going to be in the year that had hardly started. There are, of course, exceptions; someone could have had a job in 1986 and find themselves unemployed in 1987. In this case, they must notify the tax-collector with a signed and dated declaration before leaving employment. They can then elect to pay against the income they expect to have in the future. If the actual income exceeds the estimation by more than one-tenth, they will be expected to pay an increase of 10 per cent. Contrary to the practice in Britain, tax is not deducted automatically at source from the salary: there is no PAYE. It is up to the taxpayer to pay his dues directly, in one of several ways.

A) Three Stage Payments (Tiers Provisionnel)

You can choose to pay by a method traditional in France – that of three stage payments. On 31 January and 30 April you pay the first two instalments of tax on your income. As on 31 January you will not yet have submitted your tax return based on what you *earned* the previous year, these instalments are calculated on what taxes you *paid* that year. Each of these instalments is equal to a third of the tax paid the preceding year. The final 'third' (tiers), paid in September, represents the balance. The taxman, by now aware of your income for the previous year, increases or diminishes your third instalment, according to whether you have earned more or less in the preceding year than in the year before that.

For instance, in January and April 1987 you would pay a third each time of what you paid in total in 1986. You would, in fact, be taxed on what you had earned in 1985.

In September 1987, the taxman would ask you to pay the final third, with an increase or decrease according to whether in 1986 your income had increased or decreased in relation to 1985. If, in 1986 you had earned 10 per cent more than in 1985, the taxman would add the amount due on this extra 10 per cent income to the final instalment.

B) Monthly Payments

To avoid having to pay large sums which might dig a large hole in your monthly budget three times a year, you can elect to pay monthly. On the eighth of each month, from January to October, your bank account will be debited by one-tenth of the tax paid in the previous year. If the taxman finds that you owe less for this year than for the previous one, he will stop the payments when he has received the full amount due. On the other hand if he establishes that you owe him more than in the previous year, then the amount still due will be deducted on 8 November and 8 December.

It is up to you to decide which method of payment you prefer. Monthly payments give peace of mind. There is no danger of paying late and risking a fine, equal to an extra 10 per cent of your tax for the whole year.

However, if you are one of those people capable of planning and programming your budget, once you have paid your September instalment you can invest the money which will be due for the first third of the following year and only withdraw it from the bank on 15 February, thus benefitting from five months interest. Those who can manage it can invest double the amount, covering the period up to 15 May (your payment dates for the first two thirds are officially 31 January and 30 April, but the taxman always gives you two weeks grace!).

As in Britain, there is always a minimum income below which a person is not liable for tax. At the moment this is 34,500 Fr. (about £3,450) a year or 37,600 Fr. (£3,760) for people aged over 65. The main difference between the French and British systems is that in France the lowest rate of tax is not 27 per cent of the income. It starts at 5 per cent for the lowest incomes and goes up in stages of 5 per cent to reach 65 per cent for incomes above 460,000 Fr. (£46,000) a year.

Tax and The Family

The role your family plays when calculating your taxable income is also particular to France. Starting with one important detail: the tax return can be completed by either of two married people but it must be signed by *both*. This means that if a tax return contains some irregularities, neither party can plead ignorance. It also means that each party knows exactly what the other's taxable income is.

Generally, if a couple are both working, their incomes are declared jointly. This means they can benefit from the 'family quota' (*Le Quotient Familial*). In the taxman's eyes, the members of a family represent 'sections'. Taxpayers have the right to divide their income by a very precise number of sections depending on their family situation. People living alone without dependents (single, widowed etc) represent one single section. They are therefore taxed on the whole of their income – after deduction of the various rebates for which they are eligible (professional expenses etc.). A married couple are considered as two complete 'sections', even if both work. Their joint income (whether single or double) will then be divided by two. The first two children count as a half-section each. From the third child onwards, to encourage larger families, children count as a complete section.

Here are a few detailed examples (based on figures for 1987). On an annual income of 100,000 Fr. (£10,000):

- a single person (i.e. 1 section) will pay 22,257 Fr. income tax
- a married couple with no children (2 sections) will pay 11,172Fr.
- a married couple with one child (2.5 sections) will pay 8,446Fr.
- a married couple with 2 children (3 sections) will pay 6,757Fr.
- a married couple with 2 children and an elderly dependent relative (3.5 sections) will pay 5,149Fr.
- a couple with 4 children (4 sections) will pay 3,977Fr.

In general, you will notice that income tax in France is not as high as in Britain. The preceding example is typical: for an annual income of £10,000, the highest rate of tax is equal to 22.25 per cent whereas in Britain the minimum rate is 27 per cent.

Your lawyer or financial advisor will explain exactly how to fill in your tax return, what details of your life-style must be mentioned (the insistence of the taxman on 'outward signs of wealth' like yachts or Rolls Royces explains why French fortunes are rarely flaunted) how to work out the source of your income (agricultural, real-estate, wages) and all other points which will vary according to each specific case.

Income Tax and Housing

To get back to our main subject, i.e. housing, from 1987, the government, keen to encourage house-building, is allowing reductions in income tax for people buying new houses. If you buy a new house, financed with loans acquired after June 1986, your income tax will be reduced by 25 per cent of the amount of interest paid, up to a ceiling. You will be eligible for this reduction for the first five annual repayments.

The maximum amount of annual interest eligible for a tax reduction is:

30,000 Fr. (£3,000) for a married couple
15,000 Fr. (£1,500) for a single person

This is increased by:

2,000 Fr. (£200) for each dependent
2,500 Fr. (£250) for the second child
3,000 Fr. (£300) per third and subsequent children

For example, take a couple with two children who have to pay 60,000 Fr. (£6,000) interest on their loan for the first year. They are eligible for a tax reduction on the following amount:

30,000 Fr. + 2,000 Fr. + 2,500 Fr. = 34,500 Fr. (£3,450)

They will save 25 per cent of this sum, i.e. 8,625 Fr. (£862).

Alternatively, if you buy or build a new house and commit yourself to renting it out for at least six years, you will benefit from a double tax allowance.

1. Your income tax will be reduced by a sum equal to 10 per cent of the investment, up to a limit of 400,000 Fr. (£40,000) for a married couple and 200,000 Fr. (£20,000) for a single person.

For example, if you are married and buy, or build, a house worth 500,000 Fr. (£50,000) the maximum amount eligible for a tax reduction is 400,000 Fr. (£40,000). The reduction will then be 10 per cent of this sum, that is 40,000 Fr. (£4,000).

2. The gross income you receive from renting will, for tax calculation purposes, be reduced by 35 per cent over 10 years starting from the first rental. This deduction is added to the deduction for general expenses (outgoings, upkeep, interest on loans etc.).

For example:

annual rent:	30,000 Fr. (£3,000)
– general expenses:	9,500 Fr. (£950)
– 35 per cent:	10,500 Fr. (£1,050)
=net taxable rent income:	10,500 Fr. (£1,050)

VAT

There are four different rates of VAT (*la taxe à la valeur ajoutée* – TVA), according to the kinds of products or services concerned:

- 5.5 per cent on agricultural and food products
- 7.0 per cent on books, medicines, basic hotels, travel and entertainment (theatre, cinema etc.)
- 18.6 per cent, standard rate
- 33.3 per cent on so-called luxury goods (furs, jewelry, tobacco etc.) and pornography

CAPITAL GAINS TAX

Contrary to what happens in Britain capital gains tax (*l'impôt sur les plus-values*) in France applies to all those who have assets in French territory, even if it is not their tax address.

First and foremost, it is the sale of a house or a plot of land which concerns us here. (It's true that the French Stock Exchange is interesting for City financiers at the moment, but, for mere mortals, it is certainly less attractive than the London one.) Capital gains tax on a house varies according to whether it is a main or a secondary residence.

Main Residences

Generally capital gains tax does not apply to main residences. Exemption is granted automatically if the house has been the owner's main residence since it was bought or for at least five years. No such length of time is required when the sale is due to a family problem or a change of place or country of residence.

Secondary Residences

Regarding the second home (holiday home etc.), capital gains tax is more important if the property was bought less than two years before it was up for resale. If it was bought more than two years previously, tax is calculated on the basis of a series of scales linked with inflation, family quota and so on – all rather complicated and different for each individual.

The same rules apply on the whole for building plots. In any case, it would be madness to try and work out this tax without the help of an expert.

VAT is added to capital gains tax in some cases. This applies (a) if you sell a house that is not finished or (b) if you sell the house in the five years following its completion. VAT must be included in the price of sale that you submit to prospective buyers. You cannot inform them at the last moment that they will have to pay VAT extra.

It is also wise to check very carefully if you are thinking of buying a property in France through a foreign-based company. This can in certain cases prove useful on condition that you submit all required administrative and legal details about the company in question to the French tax authorities. There was so much abusive practice in the past that the treasury have become very suspicious and if there is the slightest shadow of doubt, they may well impose extra taxation, leaving you to prove your innocence and get your money back.

LOCAL TAXES

Rates

Rates (*la taxe d'habitation*) are payable by everyone who occupies a property, whether they own or rent it. As here, rates are calculated by local authorities. They pay for community services – street lighting, road sweeping, local schools etc. If your house in France is your main residence, you should check whether you qualify for a reduction or even an exemption, especially if you are retired or if a member of your family is elderly or handicapped.

This tax is payable on 1 January precisely. If you move in even 24 hours later, it is your predecessor who will have to pay the tax. Unlike income tax, rates are paid all at the one time.

Land Tax (Taxe Foncière)

Land tax is payable on all plots, whether they are built on or not, unless the buildings are meant for agricultural or religious use. It is not payable for two years after building or restoration of a property and sometimes for even longer in some specific cases, especially new buildings. Land tax must be paid by the owners, whether or not they are occupying or cultivating it. It is not usually a very heavy tax.

Generally, local taxes are calculated on the basis of the rental value of a property or plot of land; not its actual value but its theoretical value in an 'ideal market' situation. If you think that you are paying too much local tax you have the right, every year, to check and contest this 'theoretical value'.

DEATH DUTIES (Droits de Succession)

In France, death duties vary according to the family ties between the deceased and his heirs. In other words, the closer the relatives (beginning with the spouse) the less duties they have to pay. Quite logically, it follows that death duties are paid separately by each heir on his part of the inheritance and are not calculated at the outset on the whole estate.

Death duties are applicable to *all* the assets of a person whose tax residence is in France – as with income tax. This includes assets they may have had abroad.

If the tax address is not in France but there are assets in the country, those assets are subject to French death duties. They must, nevertheless be declared in Britain. Thanks to the joint tax convention, heirs who have had to pay duties on French assets can ask to be reimbursed by their own authorities.

Death duties for all those whose tax address is in France apply as follows.

Spouse

An automatic non-taxable allowance of 275,000 Fr. (£27,500) and then up to:

50,000 Fr.(£5,000) – 5 per cent death duties
100,000 Fr.(£10,000) – 10 per cent death duties
200,000 Fr. (£20,000) – 15 per cent death duties
3.4 million Fr. (£340,000) – 20 per cent death duties
5.6 million Fr. (£560,000) – 30 per cent death duties
11.2 million Fr. (£1,120,000) – 35 per cent death duties
over that – 40 per cent death duties

Direct Ascendents and Descendants (up to Grandchildren)

An automatic non-taxable allowance of 275,000 Fr. then up to:

50,000 Fr. (£5,000) – 5 per cent death duties
75,000 Fr. (£7,500) – 10 per cent death duties
100,000 Fr. (£10,000) – 15 per cent death duties
3.4 million Fr. (£340,000) – 20 per cent death duties
5.6 million Fr. (£560,000) – 30 per cent death duties
11.2 million Fr. (£1,120,000) – 35 per cent death duties
over that – 40 per cent death duties

Collateral (Brothers and Sisters)

Under certain conditions, that is if the relative: is single, widowed, divorced or separated; is over 50 years old or has a medical condition which prevents him or her from working; if they have lived with the deceased for five years before the latter's death, collaterals pay as follows:

Brothers and sisters

up to 150,000 Fr. (£15,000) – 35 per cent death duty
over that – 45 per cent death duty

Relations up to the fourth degree

55 per cent death duty

Relations beyond the fourth degree

60 per cent death duty

NB The rate of duty is applied separately to each portion. In other words, in the case of a spouse, the 10 per cent rate is only applied to the sum between 50,000 Fr. and 100,000 Fr. and *not* between 0 Fr. and 100,000 Fr.

So, a widow or widower, inheriting 80,000 Fr. over and above the 275,000 Fr. allowance, will pay 5 per cent duty on 50,000 Fr. and 10 per cent on 30,000 Fr.

ROAD TAX (Vignette Automobile)

The tariff for road tax is fixed each year by the general administration department (*Conseil Général*) of each county. It varies according to the age and size (HP) of your vehicle, calculated in 'tax horse power'. On average you can expect to pay between 200 Fr. and 2,000 Fr. for a car less than five years old, depending on the power of the engine. For a vehicle more than five years old the rate is usually half. The tax is payable by 30 November at the latest, at the tobacconist's (*bureau de tabac*).

In short...
- If you reside in France more than 183 days a year, you will be considered as having your 'fiscal domicile' there and will therefore be liable to French income tax
- There is no PAYE in France. Income tax is paid three times a
- The income tax declaration must be signed by both husband and wife
- The rate of VAT in France is not the same for all goods; it varies from 5.5 per cent to 33.3 per cent
- Capital gains tax is applicable to both residents and non-residents on the sale of a property that is not their principal residence

USEFUL ADDRESSES

In London

Franco–British Chamber of Commerce
Knightsbridge House
197 Knightsbridge
London SW7 1RZ
Tel: 01-225 5250
(For addresses of Franco-British tax consultants)

In Paris

Centre des Non-Résidents
9 Rue d'Uzès
75002 Paris
Tel: 42 36 02 33

Fiscal Advice

Cabinet Sarrut Le Poittevin Jalenques
47 Avenue Hoche
75008 Paris
Tel: 47 63 45 63

7
RENTING

Many foreigners who spend a limited amount of time in France – perhaps two or three years – for educational or professional reasons opt for renting rather than buying. This solution is not necessarily ideal in countries like Britain geared more towards buying but it is much easier in France, especially in large towns.

French real estate actually includes a large proportion of rented property; this situation derives from the financial activities and habits of the country. The fundamental reason for this difference between French and British housing markets is that in France long-term leases – 99 years or more – are very rare. When an individual in London buys a flat, 9 times out of 10 he is buying not the walls but a lease of varying length and therefore with a value to match. A Parisian on the other hand is buying the bricks and mortar, with no time limit. This system means that when a French person buys a house it is usually for life, so the housing market moves very slowly. A second consequence is that speculative buying is usually confined to commercial or industrial groups (banks, insurance companies etc.), who acquire a block of flats and let them, while waiting to re-sell them later.

THE LAW

Since the housing law of December 1986, called the *loi Méhaignerie* after the minister who was responsible for it, the minimum lease for renting has been three years. There is no maximum time length and many people stay in the same flat for years and years; however, the possibility of renewing the lease at the end of three years, and at that point, renegotiating the rent, creates greater mobility and thus greater availability of housing for rental. The Méhaignerie law allows the owner to set what rent he wishes providing the price is consistent with the average rate of rent in the same area. This price cannot be changed during the term of the current lease. An annual rent increase can be applied but it must not exceed the cost-of-construction index – around 2.3 per cent in 1987.

Short-term leases are, in fact the best way for owners – individuals or groups – to make some profit from their property, otherwise they would have no reason to let and would soon turn towards the British system of short-term buying and selling. Parisians complain a lot about the cost of rented property, which they find exorbitant, but a quick comparison between housing ads in French and English newspapers is enough to show that prices in Paris are still lower than in London; as prices in the country are generally much lower than in Paris (we are not talking here about holiday renting) it is easy to understand why many British people, like everyone else, rent their flats.

Under the Socialist government, from 1981 to March 1986, the authorities enacted a law to reinforce protection for tenants and control the raising of rents; this law has since been replaced by the 'Méhaignerie' law. The latter has maintained, up to a point, protection for tenants (by preventing, in particular, premature eviction) but as far as prices are concerned it relies on supply and demand to maintain stability. After its return to power in 1988, the Socialist government brought little change to the Méhagnerie law. A couple of amendments were made; it is now compulsory for owners to justify any large raise in rent by PROVING that all they are doing is catching up with the prices of surrounding property of equivalent type and size. This documented proof must cover the price situation over the three preceding years and must be provided before the rent is raised (and not just when the irate tenant has taken the owner to law!).

By cutting taxes (see Chapter 6), for people who buy or build new houses and rent them out, the government is trying to help stabilize prices and enlarge the housing market. But in the meantime it is not quite the law of the jungle your French friends will complain about the moment you set foot in France, particularly in Paris. In any case, one of the main characteristics of tenants in France is that they are never satisfied; but then, nor are the landlords. When the Socialist law was passed everyone complained that panic-stricken landlords no longer wanted to let their properties and that it was a battle to get a place to rent; since the Méhaignerie law, tenants complain about exploitation and extortion while landlords moan because they do not find it liberal enough! But for generations, even centuries, the French have adapted very well to a system they obviously have no intention of getting rid of (bricks and mortar are as always their favourite form of investment), so we can assume that the situation is not as bad as they make out.

You will soon discover that Parisians, always true to their creed of 'do it yourself' find lodgings thanks to a real 'underground network' between friends and relations: word is spread that a property has been vacated so as to make sure it is re-let to someone they know; all this goes on with the agreement of the landlords who prefer to let their property below the price which they are entitled to ask, against the knowledge that their tenant will be 'trustworthy', will not cause any trouble and will not get involved in any legal wrangling. The efficiency and profit of this system are not obvious but those who get involved in it have the satisfaction of not having to do the same as the rest of the world.

LOOKING FOR PROPERTY

Having started by studying the situation and avoided being influenced by general pessimism, you are now ready to launch yourself into looking for a property to rent.

First of all you should know that long-term leasing applies in most cases to unfurnished properties, not furnished ones.

To find a flat or house to rent, the easiest way is to look in the local papers. Some dailies, like *le Figaro*, devote entire pages to house advertisements in Paris and the suburbs. You will soon realize that the majority of these advertisements are put in by professionals and the telephone numbers are those of estate agents. Sometimes the number is that of the property described but in 9 out of 10 cases the tenant will refer you back to the estate agent.

If you do not want to go through an estate agency, you can go to an organization called *De Particulier à Particulier* (For Private Buyers) which publishes a magazine, under the same name, full of housing advertisements. The advantage of the organization is that transactions are carried out between the landlord and tenant with no middle man. However, your choice may be more limited and you may need more time to find what you want. It all depends on the time you have available and the urgency of finding a property.

As well as looking in newspapers, you can go straight to estate agents in the districts or areas that interest you. But don't be content with telling them what you want and then waiting for them to come up with something. You run the risk of waiting a long time and being disappointed. The renting market is very changeable and there are enough people wanting homes for the estate agents to have neither the need nor the time to chase after customers who do not make the effort to contact them. It is up to you to contact the estate agent regularly if you do not want to be forgotten.

There are still very few relocation agencies in France. More are beginning to open up although they generally prefer to work with businesses rather than individuals. If your company is sending you to France, it is possible that they have a contract with one of these agencies which are mostly Anglo-Saxon and have offices in Britain. It is obviously a solution which will avoid the traumas of having to face a system you are not familiar with and to do business in a language which is not your own.

If this possibility is not open to you, you will have to get involved in the system as it is practised by everyone else. It will be in Paris that you will have the most difficulty. In other towns, the housing market is much less congested, to such a point that the Méhaignerie law produced no rises in rent, nor confrontations between landlord and tenant, as was the case straightaway in Paris.

If you are going to live in the capital, the first golden rule is that those who get up early get flats. If you wait till the end of the morning to look at the papers and start phoning you will find that three quarters of the properties advertised will have been reserved already. By contacting the agency as soon as possible you will get an appointment at the flat, at the same time, however, as a number of other prospective tenants. Do not be surprised to find yourself at the entrance to a block of flats with a queue of 15 or so other people, like at the post office. Obviously this is not always the situation, but it is generally best to be warned of the worst and to have a nice surprise when your visit to a flat is completely relaxed and pleasant!

MAKING ARRANGEMENTS

In general the renting of flats is done without a notary or lawyer being needed. The estate agent gets the owner and yourself to sign the lease, the idea being that it is quicker and simpler if you do not involve men of law. Nevertheless, you will be signing a document which binds you, legally and financially, for a long time; if you do not speak fluent French and if you are not sure of the precise wording of the document, it is essential for you to consult a lawyer.

Whatever the case, it may be useful for you to know from the start some details peculiar to the French system of renting, thus avoiding unpleasant surprises.

To start with, better take the same precautions with renting as you would with buying from an estate agent. Ask them if they belong to the FNAIM (National Federation of Estate Agents) and check whether they have a professional charter.

Next, you should know that the estate agent's fees are paid at least partly by the person renting. In general this part is equal to a minimum of a month's rent. Even before taking possession of your property, this is what you will have to pay:

- estate agent's fee (at least a month's rent)
- a deposit (two months' rent)
- a month's rent in advance

Total: four months' rent to be paid in advance, and that is the minimum. The amount can total the equivalent of six months' rent!

NB: If you pay your rent on a three monthly basis (which is not a frequent occurrence) the landlord cannot ask you for a deposit of six months' rent.

In France rent is calculated monthly, not weekly as in Britain, at least for unfurnished properties. The deposit is meant, in principle, to cover any eventual repairs or restoration that the landlord may have to do following your stay in the flat. Even if you leave the property in the exact state you took it over, you may have some difficulty in getting your deposit back. One can always find a scratch, stain or tear, which will give sufficient justification to keep two months' rent. There is nothing to prevent you from asking for copies of bills from painters, plumbers and other repairers who came in after you left; with a little luck you will get them six months later. It is all a case of who can hold out the longest.

There is a weapon you can use, however: it is called the Inventory of Fixtures (*Etat des Lieux*). This document, which comes with the rent contract, describes the exact state of the property at the time it is signed over to you. If the tenant or landlord requires, it can be drawn up and signed by a bailiff. Although this can seem long and frustrating, it is in your interest to have as detailed an inventory as possible. If one of the tiles in the kitchen is cracked, if the linoleum in the bathroom is torn, if there are nail marks in the walls, make a note of all that. In any case it is a guarantee as much for the proprietor as for you, as the law demands that you leave the property in the same state as you found it. If you think that the premises are badly in need of improvement, updating or decoration don't go ahead with the work before getting the official go-ahead from the landlord. In any case, at the end of the lease, he may sob thankfully on your shoulder but he won't repay you a penny, unless certain items of work have been officially deemed necessary at the start and the agreement of the proprietor obtained on the original estimate.

It is equally important to know that the tenant must pay for the general charges i.e. heating, upkeep of communal areas (corridors, stairs, lift etc.), security (intercoms, codes...), hygiene (putting out the dustbins, disinfecting rubbish chutes) etc. That is why, in the housing adverts, it is always clearly stated whether the rent is inclusive of charges or not.

Your deposit will be calculated on the basis of the rent *without* charges. Finally, you should know that in France when you rent an unfurnished flat it is literally unfurnished, including any electrical appliances. Apart from very modern flats where, for instance, the hob is fitted, you would normally have to provide your own cooker, refrigerator and dishwasher.

RECIPROCAL OBLIGATIONS

Under the terms of the law of 30 December 1986, landlord and tenant are subject to certain strict legal, financial and administrative obligations.

The Terms of the Rent Contract

This must be drawn up in writing and must clearly state:

- the date on which it takes effect and the length of time involved
- a description of the property and its uses (can one, for example, use all or part of the property for professional purposes?)
- the description of places and facilities of which the tenant has sole use (for example, a space in an underground car park)
- the amount of the rent, the method of payment and the rules regarding any eventual revision
- the amount of the deposit

When a block of flats is under the jurisdiction of a co-ownership scheme, the leaseholder must inform the tenant of the co-ownership rules concerning the intended purpose of the building and use of private and communal areas, and they must state clearly what charges the flat in question is liable for.

The law does not permit the leaseholder to include the following demands in the contract (if they appear they are considered null and void):

- a clause stating that the tenant will make the property available for visiting on Bank Holidays or for more than two hours on other days, if the property is up for sale or for letting
- a clause making the tenant take out insurance with a company chosen by the leaseholder
- a clause demanding payment of rent by standing order, bank draft or bill of exchange
- preliminary commitment by the tenant to pay repair bills based on a single, one-sided estimate obtained by the leaseholder
- a clause allowing the leaseholder to demand fines if, for example a rule has been broken within the building. So, if you have an animal in a flat where animals are forbidden – which is very rare – it is out of the question to make you pay a fine to the owner or co-owners
- a ban on the tenant carrying out political, social, trade union or religious activities

The Length of the Rent Contract

The contract is drawn up for a period of at least three years. The length of time for notice to quit is three months on the side of the tenant and six months on the side of the landlord. However, in the case of a change or loss of job the tenant can give one month's notice. The notice must be served by registered letter together with a receipt (very important as you must have proof that it was sent) or by a deed from a bailiff. If notice has been served by the leaseholder, the tenant is liable for rent only for the time he or she has actually occupied the premises. In other words, if you find another flat and you move out before the six months notice has expired, you do not have to pay after you have left the premises. If the tenants have given notice, on the other hand, they are liable for rent and charges during the whole period of notice – even if they are no longer there – unless, with the agreement of the leaseholder, another tenant has moved in.

If the leaseholder and tenant agree to renew the contract at the end of three years (and they must do this at least three months before the previous contract expires) the contract is renewed for a similar period of three years minimum.

In the event of non-agreement during these three months, the proposition to renew the contract reverts to a notice to quit. In the event of no proposition to renew the contract or notice to quit, the rent contract which has run to term is considered by law to be automatically renewed 'by tacit agreement' for a further three years.

When a particular event causes the owner to take back the property for professional or family reasons (returning from a post abroad, or as a present to an offspring who is getting married), it is possible to terminate a contract in less than three years. But this must be after at least one year and the contract must mention the reasons for the short terms. The owner is then obliged to confirm the reasons at least two months before the end of the contract. As there are often unforeseen changes of circumstances it is possible that the event requiring the departure of the tenant does not happen. In this case, the owner must warn the tenant at least two months before the end of the contract and can offer a new lease for a year. However, this option can only be used once. If, at the end of the second year, the expected event has still not happened, the law automatically transfers the tenant's contract to a three year lease.

Take care: the three years commence when the very first contract is signed, so, if the contract, at the end of two years, automatically becomes a three year lease, that only leaves one year before the tenant's lease expires. It is quite evident that an unscrupulous proprietor must not invent an 'engagement' of an offspring in order to limit you to a one-year lease and then 'break off' the engagement at the end of a year so as to offer you a renewed lease – at a new price. If you sign a year's lease it is wise to check that there is a clause which prevents your landlord from merrily adding another 50 per cent to the rent in the event of an unexpected renewal of lease at the end of one year.

THE TENANT'S OBLIGATIONS

The tenant must:

- pay the rent and service charges on the agreed terms; if the tenant prefers and requests a monthly rent, his right prevails
- use the premises in a quiet manner and for the purpose intended
- be responsible for all damage and losses incurred during the length of his stay, unless he can prove that they were caused by circumstances outside his control, by the fault of the leaseholder or by a third party whom the tenant did not invite into the property (a burglar for example)
- take upon himself the regular maintenance of the property including repairs incumbent upon the tenant (specified by an official order), unless these repairs are due to age, bad workmanship or construction faults, or to circumstances outside his control
- allow the carrying out of repair work to the public areas of the building, the private premises of other occupants and also such work as is necessary to keep his own flat well maintained and in good order. (If the owners or co-owners decide to install gas central heating instead of oil, the tenant cannot prevent it, especially as the proprietor is paying)
- avoid changes in the premises or fixtures without the written permission of the landlord
- insure against any risks for which they are liable as tenant

As a tenant, you are not allowed to transfer your contract or to sublet the premises without the written agreement of the leaseholder, which must state the terms of the sub-letting.

THE OWNER'S OR LEASEHOLDER'S OBLIGATIONS

The owner or the leaseholder must:

- hand over the property in a state of good repair and ready for use, including all fixtures and fittings in working order. If some repair work is necessary and has not been carried out by the time the contract is signed there can be a clause describing this work and its effect on the rent
- assure the tenant a quiet existence in the property and guarantee against faults and defects capable of disrupting the tenant's peaceful existence, with the exception of those repairs already mentioned in the contract
- maintain the premises in a state suitable for the use defined in the contract and carry out all repairs necessary for maintaining the property in an acceptable state
- not oppose improvements carried out by the tenant as long as it does not mean a complete transformation of the property.

NB: All these points apply to the renting of *unfurnished* flats. They do not apply to furnished flats: on the one hand they are far fewer and on the other hand they are often let to people who do not stay in them very long. It is therefore impossible to impose three-year leases. Each furnished letting is the subject of an individual contract. For those who wish to stay a short time in Paris, but do not want to go to a hotel there are organizations that let flats of all sizes for differing lengths of time. You will find a list at the end of this chapter but you can equally well obtain one yourself by contacting the French Government Tourist Office (*L'Office National Français Du Tourisme*) in London.

It should also be noted that the Méhaignerie law does not change the system as it applies to HLMs (*Habitation à Loyer Modéré* – the equivalent of council houses); the State has imposed a minimum and maximum scale for these properties and any increase must be agreed to by the authorities.

LETTING YOUR PROPERTY

It is possible that you own a property in France and want to let it. If you let the property unfurnished it is obvious that the Méhaignerie law will affect you directly as leaseholder.

However, there is a good chance that your property will be furnished – because it is either a holiday home or a base in town. In this case you probably do not want to rent it for very long periods during which you will not have access. You will have to contact an organization which specializes in this type of letting. If you do not know of an agency locally which you can trust, here too it would be worth your while obtaining a list of specialist British agencies from the French Tourist Office.

If you have a villa at the seaside or a chalet in the mountains and you want to let it for a long period, do not forget that you cannot ask the kind of rent you would expect if you were only letting it in the holiday season. If you know that you will not be in France for a long time, you are quite within your rights to let your property during the time you are not there, but make certain that the exact period is written into the contract.

In general it would seem better for you to put a few pieces of furniture of little value into your property and to let it as furnished since this will give you much more flexibility in the length of the lease.

In the table are some average monthly prices (excluding service charges) for renting in Paris, in 1987.

District	*Arrdt*	*One-roomed flat* $22–34\ m^2$	*Five-roomed flat* $100–130\ m^2$
Opéra	1st	2,200–3,200Fr	7,500–10,000Fr
Halles	2nd	1,700–2,500Fr	5,700–7,500Fr
Marais	3rd	2,000–2,800Fr	6,500–9,000Fr
Saint-Louis	4th	2,700–4,000Fr	6,000–16,000Fr
Sorbonne	5th	2,100–3,000Fr	7,000–13,000Fr
Luxembourg	6th	2,200–4,000Fr	7,500–16,000Fr
Eiffel T	7th	2,300–4,000Fr	8,000–18,000Fr
Ch. Elysées	8th	1,900–4,000Fr	6,000–15,000Fr
Haussmann	9th	1,600–2,700Fr	4,800–8,000Fr
Magenta	10th	1,600–2,300Fr	4,600–6,000Fr
République	11th	1,700–2,400Fr	4,800–6,500Fr

Nation	12th	1,600–2,600Fr	4,600–7,000Fr
Gobelins	13th	1,600–2,600Fr	3,800–7,000Fr
Montsouris	14th	1,700–3,500Fr	4,700–9,500Fr
Montparnasse	15th	1,900–3,200Fr	5,000–9,500Fr
Etoile	16th	2,100–4,000Fr	6,500–16,000Fr
Monceau	17th	1,700–3,500Fr	4,800–13,000Fr
Montmartre	18th	1,600–2,800Fr	3,800–9,000Fr
Buttes Chaumont	19th	1,600–2,800Fr	3,800–9,000Fr
Père Lachaise	20th	1,600–2,200Fr	4,200–5,700Fr

In short...

- For long-term rental, most properties are not furnished

- Leases are usually signed for three years and tacitly renewed for another three years if both parties are satisfied with the current position

- If you are renting a property:
  - ask the agent if he belongs to the FNAIM;
  - be very firm when it comes to the official description of the state of the lodging and insist on adding any detail you consider necessary;
  - ask a bilingual solicitor to go over your contract to make sure that you are as fully protected as possible

- A tenant cannot make any structural changes to the property without his landlord's agreement

- When you decide to leave, you must warn your landlord three months in advance by *registered* letter

USEFUL ADDRESSES

Fédération Nationale des Agents
Immobiliers et Mandataires
(FNAIM)
129 Rue du Faubourg St Honoré
75008 Paris
Tel: 42 25 24 26

Confédération Nationale du
Logement
62 bis Boulevard Richard-Lenoir
75011 Paris
Tel: 47 00 96 20
  • (Defence of tenants' rights)

Centre d'Information Logement
204 Rue Lecourbe
75015 Paris
Tel: 45 31 14 50

Flat Rental for Short Stays In Paris

Résidence La Fontaine
2 Rue Saint-Lazare
75009 Paris
Tel: (1) 48 78 32 86
  • weekly or monthly rental
    studios near opéra

Lovac
48 Rue des Acacias
75017 Paris
Tel: 43 80 15 06
Tx: 650 794
  • minimum rental one week,
    maximum three months
  • studios and apartments

Résidences Orion
39 Rue de Surèue
75008 Paris
Tel: 42 66 33 26
  • private parking
  • studios/apartments at les
    Halles, Pont de Nevilly, La
    Défense
  • daily, weekly or monthly
    rental

Résidences Pierre et Vacances
54 Avenue Marceau
75008 Paris
Tel: 47 20 70 87
  Tx: 613 778
  • parking facilities if required
  • daily, weekly or monthly
    rental
  • studios and apartments

Flatotel International
14 Rue du Theâtre
75015 Paris
Tel: 45 75 62 20
Tx: 200 406
- studios, apartments
- daily, weekly, monthly
  rental

Residence du Roy
8 Rue François-ler
75008 Paris
Tel: 42 89 59 59
Tx: 648 452
- studio and apartments
- daily, weekly and monthly
  rentals

Residence Bassano
15 Rue de Bassano
75116 Paris
Tel:47 23 78 23
Tx: 649 872

Residence Le Claridge
74 Champs-Elysées
75008 Paris
Tel: 43 59 67 97
Tx: 290 548
- studios and apartments
- monthly rentals

Paris Flat Service Gestion
6 Rue du Dr-Finlay
750015 Paris
Tel: 45 79 64 03
Tx: 202 028
- modern tower block by river
  Seine
- studios and apartments
- weekly or monthly rentals

Citadines Paris-Austerlitz
27 Rue Esquirol
75013 Paris
Tel: 45 84 13 09
- daily, weekly or monthly
  rentals
- studios and apartments

Elysees Concorde
9 Rue Royale
75008 Paris
Tel: 42 65 11 99
Tx: 640 793
- weekly or longer rentals
- baby-sitting facilities
- studios and apartments near
  les Invalides or Avenue
  Foch

France Ermitage
MJC Frebour
5 Rue Berryer
75008 Paris
Tel: 42 56 23 42
- studios and 2-room
  apartments

Locaflat
193 Boulevard Brune
75014 Paris
Tel: 43 06 78 79
Tx: 250 302
- 5 days min., monthly or 3 months
- apartments and studios in Paris 14e and 15e

Paris Sejour Reservation
90 Avenue des Champs-Elysées
75008 Paris
Tel: 42 56 30 00
Tx: 643 945
- apartments and studios
- daily, weekly, monthly or yearly rentals

8
HOLIDAY VISITS

Obviously the vast majority of British people don't go to France intending to spend the rest of their days, or even several years there, but simply their holidays.

According to official statistics one in four Britons going abroad chooses France as his destination. The type of accommodation chosen by the British varies considerably, although half of them opt for a hotel. There are so many different options open to tourists that entire books are regularly devoted to the subject. We shall, therefore, limit ourselves to describing the types of holiday directly linked to the central theme of this book, that is to say dwellings – buildings with walls and a roof in contrast to tents, caravans and motor homes. As far as hotels are concerned, the only ones mentioned here will be the *Logis de France* hotels, because they are notably popular with British tourists.

So, you have decided to spend a month, a fortnight, or a week (according to the season) in France, but you don't want to go on a package tour, pay hotel costs for a family, or let your mother-in-law get rheumatism from sleeping in a tent. There is certainly no shortage of specialist agencies in Britain and France. The real problem is choosing what suits you.

Your first logical step should be to follow the example of your fellow countrymen: every year at least half a million of them contact the French Government Tourist Board in London. It is a very reliable organization, established since 1920, which makes it along with the Barcelona and Geneva Tourist Boards, the oldest one in London. It can boast the most important information service of all the 60 or so foreign tourist offices in the capital. Seven information officers are on hand to answer queries, by telephone, in writing, or in person to those who go to 178 Piccadilly. With the 2,000 brochures and pamphlets and 150 annual tons of paperwork provided by the Office, you should have no difficulty finding what you want!

At the outset, you must make two basic decisions: where do you want to go and what type of holiday best suits your tastes and personal situation?

The three regions preferred by British tourists are Brittany, the Riviera and the Dordogne. Paris and the Ile de France are equally popular, but more for short stays: cultural trips rather than long family holidays. You will also have to decide whether you want to move around or stay put.

TOURING

Logis de France

Those who wish to tour can choose a hotel, which, as already stated, is popular with many British people (when you compare the prices with those in the UK you understand why!). One of the best known organizations is the *Logis et Auberges de France*. This is not an agency, but an association which groups some 5,000 hotels across France offering good quality and good value.

To earn the right to display the coveted sign of the *Logis de France* (a fire burning in a hearth), hotels are subjected to very strict rules of comfort, hygiene, service, quality of food (gastronomy) ... and price. They are mostly one or two star hotels, in attractive locations, with prices ranging from £5 to £12 a day (for two) including breakfast or even half-board. You must book directly with the hotel but the London Tourist Board will send you the free brochure of the Logis if you send an S.A.E. (for 50p).

Chambre d'Hôtes

Another solution, fairly recent but equally suitable for those who don't want to spend more than a night or two in the same place, are the *Chambres d'Hôtes*. These have been modelled on the British bed and breakfast tradition, and that is exactly what is on offer: a room with a bathroom plus breakfast, in a private house. This organization is under the sponsorship of the *Gîtes de France* who also take care of the *Gîtes Ruraux* so popular with the British (see further on).

Foreigners often complain that the French don't give them a very warm welcome. The first thing you will discover with the *Chambres d'Hôtes* is that, when the French do open their homes to you, they also open their hearts. It will be an ideal occasion to involve yourself, even for a short while, in the lives of people from all sorts of social and professional backgrounds, whose aim in opening up their house to passing strangers is not to make a fortune (as is obvious from the modest charges) but to make new friends.

The range is varied: you can go from a cottage in Normandy to a manor in Brittany, from a *château* in Sologne to a farm in Haute Provence. But wherever you go, if you can speak two or three words of French (or your hosts two or three words of English) you can expect, in addition to buttered slices of fresh bread and bowls of coffee at breakfast, a very friendly conversation. Obviously, if you wish to spend your breakfast with your nose in your cup or behind your road map, they will avoid disturbing you, but if such is the case, and contact with the locals does not interest you, you may be better off at a hotel...

The *Chambres d'Hôtes* (guest houses) have to observe strict rules of hygiene and are subject to regular visits from qualified inspectors.

There are other similar organizations, for instance: *Caf Couette*.

Café Couette

This is an organization created along the same lines as the *Chambres d'Hôtes*. The people who belong to it are not professional 'renters' like the famous landladies of English seaside resorts: sometimes the money from letting rooms allows them to keep a pretty family home they would otherwise have to sell; more often, it gives them a chance to see a bit of the outside world in the course of a quiet and perhaps rather monotonous life in the country. They consider you very sincerely as paying guests with emphasis on the word 'guests'. With *Caf Couette*, on top of breakfast you can have other meals during the day depending on your host's availability. At the family table you will get to know about the things of interest to see in the surrounding area, what to avoid etc., in a much livelier way than by reading your guide-book. A *Caf Couette* book with a list of prices and addresses is available.

Demeures Club

This is an organization which groups 40 or so historical dwellings whose owners, there again, treat you like personal guests.

Châteaux en Vacances

Again the same idea but here you are assured of a place in a *château* and can expect to take part in the life of the occupants.

If holidays in a *château* attract you there are also British agencies specializing in this type of accommodation. You will find the list in the Tourist Board's annual *Guide for the Traveller in France*.

'STAYING PUT'

Exchanges

If the idea of spending your holidays in a private house in France interests you, you might consider an exchange. This method has the advantage of not costing too much and has in many cases allowed French and English families to forge long-lasting links of friendship. It involves spending an agreed period in a house in France while the inhabitants come and spend their holidays in your house. The organizations which specialize in this kind of business take good care to put in touch families in the same financial bracket, with ages and life-styles as compatible as possible. This way the interested parties stand a chance of getting on well together.

Villages-Vacances-Familles

Holidays which are not too expensive and have been going for a long time in France are now available to foreigners through the family holiday villages (*Villages-Vacances-Familles*). These are run by a non-profit making association, created in 1958 to allow low income families to spend holidays they would not otherwise be able to afford. There are 126 holiday villages across France, with a capacity of 64,000 beds, that take in 550,000 holidaymakers every year.

More than half these villages are by the sea, the rest are scattered between the mountains and the countryside. The land and the buildings belong to the local communities and public authorities, which keeps prices at modest levels. Most offer flats or bungalows, with small areas reserved for camping and caravanning.

The advantage of these villages is that they offer child-minding and entertainment for children and young people, leaving parents free to relax in peace and make the most of their holiday. They also welcome groups of young people and teenagers as well as elderly or handicapped people.

VVF is the best known group but there are others; you will find them in brochures dealing with a particular region or department. If, for example, you have chosen to spend your holidays in Normandy, the Tourist Board will provide a brochure on the region containing a list of: holiday villages, family holiday homes, villages of *gîtes*, addresses of organizations where you can rent a farmhouse; estate agents who can offer seasonal rentals, and finally tourist and information offices offering a list of furnished accommodation in their area. What is true for Normandy is of course equally true for other regions of France.

The formula of holiday villages has been pursued with great success by an organization known throughout the world, the *Club Méditerranée*. The Club Med. now has villages the world over offering a whole range of activities, mainly sporting, which vary according to the area. There are several villages in France. However, whereas the Club has been a great success where the French are concerned, this has not really been the case with the British, perhaps because, for the same cost, they would prefer quieter and more exclusive holidays.

Gîtes

Gîte is a word that comes up frequently in brochures and handbooks – and for a very good reason. It is by far the method of self-catering holidays in France that the British prefer. In 1977 the *Fédération Nationale des Gîtes Ruraux* set up, at 178 Piccadilly, an office to promote and commercialize this unusual and homely way of renting out property in the French countryside. It's known as *Gîtes de France*.

The *Gîtes* are privately owned properties – a farm, a house in a village, a manor, or a chalet – modernized with the help of government grants and under the auspices of the *Gîtes Ruraux*, a non-profit making association. A *gîte* is let to holidaymakers as a self-catering unit at a very attractive price. For a cottage or flat within a house the average price is £80–£95 a week for four people in high season (July–August) and £50–£75 out of season. For a stay including the return fare on the Dover–Calais car ferry, it will cost about £175 a week for two adults and two children in May and October or £282 for two weeks in September, taking the Portsmouth–Cherbourg crossing.

For the last 10 years the *Gîtes de France* have enjoyed spectacular success in Britain: from the 300 *gîtes* available in 1977 the number has increased to 2,000 today; during this same period the lettings have gone from 600 to 10,000 a year. Thirty thousand copies of the English directory are published each year.

To rent a *gîte* you must become a member of the Federation, for the modest sum of £3. This entitles you to the *Guide des Gîtes* as well as another guide, entitled *Loisirs-Accueil*, which offers a whole list of other options for holidays in rural France (small hotels, specialist holidays, sporting holidays etc.).

NB: You can also obtain a list of *Chambres d'Hôtes* and *Logis de France* by contacting the *Gîtes de France*. You can equally find lists of *gîtes* in the brochures published by the regional tourist offices (and distributed to the FGTO and travel agents in this country). Regional brochures have the advantage of including colour photographs, which are more attractive. In any case, you will discover that what is not under the label *Gîtes de France* will go under that of *Loisirs-Accueil*.

To reserve from *Loisirs-Accueil* you have several options: go through a British travel agent, apply to the Tourist Board in London or even contact the offices of the organization in the region you are interested in. In general, these offices don't ask for fees and have someone there who speaks English.

Seaside and Mountain Holidays

Those who prefer to spend their holidays not in the country, but at a resort by the sea or in the mountains, where life is certainly much more lively and hectic and where the possibilities for organized activities are greater, will not be attracted by *gîtes*. If you would rather rent a flat or villa by the sea or a chalet in the mountains, there are several ways of organizing your holiday.

You can leave everything, from booking ferry tickets to renting a flat, including one or two nights in a hotel on the way there, to a travel organization like French Leave, which can be contacted through its offices in London or your local travel agent. Prices vary according to the location and types of accommodation.

In the same vein, you can contact an organization which specializes in the letting of flats, houses or hotel rooms in specific holiday resorts: a group like Maeva offers a range of different types of accommodation (hotels, *club résidences*, flats) in eight winter sports resorts and in six seaside resorts or towns. There too, the prices vary according to the type of accommodation and the date of your holiday.

Another possibility is to get a list of places to rent in specific locations from the Tourist Board. There is for instance a guide to seasonal renting in Charente-Maritime, called *Locacharente*. All the places mentioned in the guide have been visited and classified by the local tourist authorities. Once you have chosen a suitable place and accommodation, you telephone *Locacharente* to get all the relevant details and to check that it is available. It's always best to make a short list of properties which attract you: with one phone call to *Locacharente* you will know straightaway which are still available instead of ringing each individual owner. Once you have made your choice, then you can ring the owner or the estate agent and finalize the details for your stay.

Another organization worth recommending is *Allo Vacances* – a branch of the FNAIM (National Federation of Estate Agents) listing all the agencies that offer self-catering holidays. You are certain to be doing business with reputable people (not cowboys) committed to observing the laws on housing, in agreement with the public authorities. *Allo Vacances*'s catalogue supplies you with a list of agencies throughout France, as well as a form to fill in and send to the agency of your choice in the area you prefer. You can make your booking either directly through the agency or (if you see things you like at several agents) by calling central reservations (*Centrale de Réservation*) in Paris, who will tell you what is still available on your list and who will do the final booking.

Going It Alone

Finally, there is nothing to stop you doing it all yourself on the spot, by arranging your forthcoming holiday accommodation with a local agency or directly with the owner of a property which suits you. But be very careful: unless you are a regular visitor to the place, and have complete confidence in the locals, you may risk having some unpleasant surprises which will spoil your holiday.

For instance, are you sure of having legal protection if the owner backs out a few days before you are due to arrive, leaving you to find alternative accommodation at short notice?

There are also some 'minor' details like the insurance, in case of accident or damage. If the gas stove blows up in your face, you risk spending not only days in hospital but months in court to obtain compensation. In agreements between private individuals, there can be oversights or grey areas which mean serious problems in case of accidents. The alternative is to have the contract verified by solicitors – a bit over the top for a 2-week holiday in the country! With a serious, well known company this kind of problem is anticipated.

As an example, *Gîtes de France* have you automatically insured with Norwich Union (unless you opt out specifically) for the entire holiday (including the trip) against: accident, illness, theft or loss of personal effects, cancellation or curtailment, third-party damages, and delays on the journey. You are also entitled to the services of *Europ-Assistance* which guarantees emergency medical treatment and repatriation where necessary.

If you still prefer to do the renting yourself, there are several important points you should note before you sign the contract, to avoid unpleasant surprises.

Seasonal renting, as the name suggests, applies for a limited period of time which must not exceed 90 days. At the time of booking you may be asked for a deposit, either *des arrhes* or *un acompte* (two different things). This sum cannot be requested more than six months in advance and cannot exceed 25 per cent of the rental charge. If you pay the deposit called *arrhes*, both you and the owner can back out of the agreement; in which case you lose the sum you have paid, if *you* have backed out, but if the *owner* backs out he must pay you double. The *acompte* deposit signifies that the contract has been firmly agreed and the tenant who backs out of such an agreement is liable for the total sum of the rent.

If you are asked for a *caution* (security), this must be paid on arrival, once you have signed the inventories and not before. There again, you should not pay more than 25 per cent of the rental charge.

If you go through an agency, they will charge a commission. Normally, the commission is paid by the owner, but you can be sure that it will be reflected in the rental charge!

Above all, don't forget to examine the inventories for fixtures and equipment, checking that everything is written down from the layout of the flat to the number of egg-cups in the sideboard.

Finally, coming back to the question of insurance, there are two points you need to know if you are going to avoid any major catastrophes:

- the owner is, as a rule, insured against fire and flood damage
- the tenant is nevertheless advised to cover him or herself by taking out an 'all risks' policy for the period involved

Time-Sharing

This system has been in existence in our countries for a good 20 years or more, so its advantages and disadvantages are now pretty well known. Basically, you are buying the right to spend a limited time each year in a specific property, usually situated in a holiday resort in the mountains or by the sea.

The advantage of the system is that you have access to a kind of 'second home', where you can return regularly without having to pay the full purchase price or having to concern yourself with the day-to-day problems of owning a property. You can, if you wish, sell your rights back to the property company if you have had enough of going back to the same place year after year, or if you like the resort so much that you want to buy something permanent.

However, any lawyer will tell you that the system requires careful consideration, in whichever country it is operating. Here also, make sure you are dealing with organizations you can trust – starting with a number of British estate agents who have connections in France and who are used to the intricacies of the French housing system.

If you launch yourself into this enterprise, now is the time to consult a lawyer. Recently, French legislators have taken steps to try and protect individuals who are buying into time-share property. For a long time, the purchaser owned nothing other than a period of time and a usage, whereas the property continued to belong to the organization or person who paid for the bricks and mortar at the start. In such a situation how could you hope to have any rights when up against the real owner or to have your say about the way the building was managed or maintained?

New legislation proposes that the time-share purchaser be given the benefit of a shareholding, which would give him the right, as shareholder, to attend general meetings and to get specific demands about management and maintenance passed by vote. Of course it means being present at the meetings, not easy if you are only there two weeks a year. In that case, you have to be represented. This is a problem to take up with the salesman or failing that with your lawyer.

There are other queries you must have answers to before committing yourself. Who is responsible if there is a domestic accident? What happens if the person before you has not paid their part of the electricity bill, or if you discover there is some furniture missing and so on? We are not trying to put you off, as the principle of time-sharing itself is quite interesting; if there were only disadvantages the system would have been abandoned long ago. However, it would be rash to launch yourself into such an operation without expert legal advice providing all possible safeguards, with regard to the French but also with regard to any British-based sales company.

In short...

• A holiday or short-term rental can last no longer than 90 days

• When booking lodgings, don't pay more than 25 per cent of total rent in advance

• Make sure that any damage or imperfection existing before you move in is mentioned in the official description of the state of the lodging; make sure that the inventory is exact

• You will need to take out house insurance for the time you are staying at your holiday lodging

USEFUL ADDRESSES

French Government Tourist
Board
178 Piccadilly
London W1V 9DB
Tel: 01-491 7622
Tx: 21902 FRANCE
(60,000 Prestel viewdata
terminals in the UK, no: 34-420)

Gîtes de France/Logis de France/
Loisirs Accueil
178 Piccadilly
London W1V 9DR
Tel: 01-493 3480

Allô Vacances FNAIM
61 Rue La Boétie
75008 Paris
Tel: 42 25 75 75

Villages Vacances Familles
33 Avenue du Maine
75015 Paris
Tel: 45 38 28 28

MAEVA
30 Rue d'Orléans
92200 Neuilly sur Seine
Tel: 47 45 17 21

Locacharentes
Comité Départemental du
Tourisme de la Charente –
Maritime
11 bis, Rue des Augustins
17008 La Rochelle
Tel: 46 41 43 33

Café Couette
8 Rue de l'Isly
75008 Paris
Tel: 42 94 92 00

Demeure Club
5 Place du March Sainte
Catherine
75004 Paris
Tel: 42 71 15 93

Châteaux en Vacances
BP 4
78220 Viroflay
Tel: 30 24 18 16

9
AROUND THE HOUSE

According to the British, there is nothing worse than French plumbing. For their part, the French consider British plumbing a national catastrophe. Don't ask us to interfere in this controversy: we shall sit firmly on top of the fence, and point out that, in general, this type of quarrel has less to do with real shortcomings on either side than with prejudices stemming from total ignorance of the techniques which run the system in each country. This is equally valid for electricity, heating, thermal insulation and all other aspects of practical living.

At first glance, a French washbasin is not very different from an English washbasin (except that the hot and cold taps are reversed), an English radiator has nothing to distinguish it from a French radiator, to the extent that the same makes are often found on both sides of the Channel. However, if you have a house renovated or built in France you will soon discover that you have to observe all sorts of rules, all kinds of technical specifications, and also take into account the geographical and climatic conditions which may be unfamiliar.

GENERAL OBSERVATIONS

For a start, the way a house is built, the materials used and the positioning of the rooms vary enormously between regions, and quite often even within regions. In Brittany, for example, you will find slate roofs all along the coast and thatched roofs inland. Much depends on the period in which the house was built, as well as on the social and financial status of the original owners. In this, France is not very different from the countries surrounding it, except that the socio-economic element brings extra variety to an already great number of very different architectural styles.

You will notice, for instance that, contrary to many preconceived ideas, all French houses do not necessarily have a cellar. Many small country houses have none. (This immediately poses the problem of rising damp, well known to the British.) Houses built at the turn of the century have exterior and partition walls which are sometimes quite thin, provide insufficient insulation against the cold and cause condensation.

You would be well advised to examine the roof timbers of your prospective property thoroughly, as there are certain regions where you find termites,particularly in the South-West, from the Loire to the Pyrenées, and on the western half of the Mediterranean coast, as well as in certain areas of Paris.

Except in the eastern regions, near Germany, and in mountain areas, the French do not install double glazing as often as the English do. There is a good reason for this: the use of shutters on the vast majority of houses. Sometimes, especially in châteaux and large private houses, the external shutters are supplemented by internal shutters fixed directly onto the window frames. You can also find detachable shutters made to cover the panes set into a door. These consist in fact, simply of a solid wood panel with two handles which slips into special hooks surrounding the glass panes. Once the door is shut, its frame prevents anyone from unhooking the shutters. Shutters have always been considered a means of security and of insulation.

The French are not generally very keen on sash windows; traditionally they tend to use casement windows. If someone explains that a house has 'English windows' (*fenêtres l'Anglaise*) they do not mean sash windows but, simply casement windows that open outwards in contrast to those that open inwards which, of course, are called 'French windows' (*à la Française*)! You will notice, indeed, that in Britain, casement windows usually open outwards.

Another typical feature of the French home is the wood burning fireplace. These are also found in Britain, of course, but they are less common, one reason being that there are fewer forests so of course less wood to burn. Of the total surface area of France 26.7 per cent is covered by forests, as against 8 per cent in Britain. As France is twice as big as Britain that makes a lot more trees to spare!

You will find a great variety of styles and sizes of fireplaces. If the one in the lounge of your future house is damaged, or if you are having a house built and want fireplaces built you will not have difficulty finding craftsmen who specialize in this type of work. It is even a trade which has become popular with young people once again. The fireplace is such a part of the French house that it would be a pity to demolish it or do without it, as craftsmen are not difficult to find.

Old houses built before 1850 tend to have open fireplaces. Then, up to the First World War, they built fireplaces housing stoves with hot-air closed flues, only to return after the War to open fireplaces. From that time on, central heating became common in France. However, it was not until 1969 that permanent ventilation of rooms became compulsory (before, people just opened the windows). Only houses built since this date have a built-in ventilation system; in others, it will have been added on... if it exists.

THERMAL INSULATION

One thing in France that foreigners do not take long to notice, is the variation in climate and temperature from region to region. Nevertheless, whatever the climate of the place where you buy your house, it is important that it should have the benefit of good thermal insulation. It would be a mistake to think that if you settle in the South of France, for example, you can avoid insulating your house. Insulation is an equally excellent protection against very great heat.

The Rules

The basic rules concerning insulation date from 1975, when it became necessary to start making serious cutbacks in energy consumption because of the increase in oil prices. Then a law passed in March 1982 called for even greater economies. To put it plainly, this means that thermal insulation in houses built before 1975 was completely haphazard; some houses have none at all.

Insulation specialists may talk to you about the 'G' coefficient. This 'Global' coefficient sets the standard degree of insulation required for a building. It is calculated by dividing the sum of heat loss by the volume of living space. The law of March 1982 states precisely what the coefficient should be, according to the characteristics of the building, the climate of the area and the type of heating used. France, for this purpose, is divided into three climatic zones: H1 (broadly speaking, the north-eastern half); H2 (the south-western half minus the Mediterranean area); H3 (the Mediterranean area and Corsica).

Calculating the G coefficient is quite complicated and you need to bring in a professional – architect, builder etc. – to find out what needs to be done for the house to conform to the legal norm. However, if the 'G coefficient' crops up in the course of a discussion, at least, you will know that it is to do with the amount of insulation needed in your particular house.

Just to make life more difficult, the 'B' coefficient has been invented; this sets out the heating needs (*Besoins*) according to the volume of the rooms and to the 'free' supply of heat (sunshine, for example). Don't think that you have finished revising the alphabet: the letter R has been chosen to denote the Resistance and efficiency of thermal insulating material. Technicians will explain that the higher the R, the more the insulation is efficient – which is quite obvious even to non-specialists!

Systems of thermal insulation in France are scarcely any different from those in Britain, whether for roofing, walls or windows.

In the event of your house having a cellar, do not forget to insulate thoroughly beneath the ground floor. Now, if you are expecting to fill your cellar with the best wines you will, of course, have to ensure that the cellar temperature does not vary to any great degree once the house has been insulated. The ideal is to have a cellar set apart from the house so as to avoid worrying about the effects of any transformation of your home!

SOUNDPROOFING

This subject will mainly concern those who are going to live in a flat or on a modern housing estate. Modern blocks of flats, as well as houses offered for building in catalogues, are subject to the 'Qualitel' index (see Chapter 3) which offers, in particular, a scale allowing you to measure the quality of the soundproofing of a building. Since 1978, if a builder wants to take advantage of the 'Soundproofing' label (*confort acoustique*) he has to guarantee sound insulation between homes, and between the home and the street, capable of absorbing a specific number of decibels. In any case, since 1977 building has been forbidden in areas which are considered very noisy.

In any case, you would be well advised to check the soundproofing of the property you are interested in with great care, especially if you are buying in the South of France. A British family runs the risk of having trouble adapting to the Mediterranean exhuberance of their next-door neighbours!

Sound Levels

In modern homes, the maximum sound levels allowed by law are 35 decibels for main rooms and 38 decibels for utility rooms. By way of comparison, the average sound levels recorded in a quiet corner of the countryside are from 20 to 30 decibels, 40 to 60 decibels in a noisy street and 80 to 100 near an airport.

Windows made today are also subjected to soundproofing tests so they can be labelled according to their airtightness and resistance to wind. Here too, the labels take into account various points like degree of exposure, types of heating and geographical situation. Every labelled window has the official emblem of the label and the degree of insulation obtained indelibly printed on it.

NB: In sunny areas, it can be useful to fit filter windows which prevent the sun's rays from overheating the glass; this is particularly useful for large picture windows. Likewise tinted panes will provide protection from the very strong light of the sun, reflected for example from the sea or the mountain snows.

You may be eligible for a tax reduction on the amount paid out for insulating your house – provided it is your principal residence. The maximum deductible expense is 7,000 francs, plus 1,000 francs for each dependent living in the house.

HEATING

There is a minor socio-economic detail which has a profound influence on heating: France has no oil. Therefore the French have learned, by force of circumstance since 1974, to economize on energy. In view of this, you, like everyone else, will be subject to the laws limiting maximum temperature within the home.

The Rules

Currently maximum legal temperatures are 19°c for living rooms and bathrooms, and 18°c for bedrooms and kitchens (no, there is no mistake: the difference is really only one degree centigrade!). For cellars, garages and lofts, the recommended temperature is 6°c to 8°c.

Obviously you are not expected to walk from room to room with a thermometer. What is required, on the other hand, is an automatic and careful regulation of your heating system. The most highly recommended system is that of individual thermostats regulated to the legal temperature in each room. This system is linked to a manual override or to a programmed time-clock. You can add a 'probe', which is a thermostat placed outside the house; this indicates the variations in the outside temperature to the heating source before the difference is noticeable within the house.

NB: Regular maintenance of your heating system must, by law, include sweeping of the flues and chimneys.

When you are choosing the type of heating you want to install, your geographical situation will play as important a role as the costs of the different systems.

Oil-fired Central Heating

Domestic heating oil has become less popular since the oil crisis; it is also becoming less competitive pricewise because it has priority use in certain industries (in the production of plastic, for example). Another problem is that you have to stock it which means having it delivered, so you have to be within reach of the distributor's lorry. Access by a mountain track in mid-winter can mean that you run the risk of not seeing the tanker for weeks on end – just at the time when you have the greatest need for heating.

Futhermore, you need to have quite a bit of space available: if the oil tank has a capacity of more than 2,000 litres, you are required by law either to bury it somewhere in your garden or to store it in a separate location sheltered from frost and away from the house. A smaller tank can be kept inside the house but you will then need to refill it several times a year, with all the inconvenience that entails.

In any case, your tank will have to be declared to the authorities, along with a certificate of testing (*Certificat d'Essai*) provided by the makers.

Gas-fired Central Heating

Gas central heating is being keenly promoted and the prices are quite competitive. It has, like electricity, the advantage of being equally usable for cooking.

You can stock up by having butane or propane gas cylinders delivered or by having a large external tank filled up (provided you can camouflage it for the sake of your neighbours!). But here too you must be careful about the problems of delivery in relation to your geographical situation.

If you can be linked up to mains gas this will at least enable you to dispense with delivery service. The price for being linked into the system can be as much as 5,000 to 6,000 francs if your house has not already been connected, but much less (not even 200 francs) if it is a case of taking over your predecessor's contract.

The distributor, Gaz de France, owns the network up to, and including, the meter, and will supervise the installation of the outside network. The meter should be placed preferably at the edge of the property or even on an outside wall of the house. It is generally read every four months. Or else, you can ask to pay a fixed sum each month; then your meter will only be read annually and your bill readjusted according to your consumption. When you are about to move in, it takes two weeks to arrange for a contract and if necessary, to fit a meter.

If you don't reside permanently in France it will no doubt be preferable for you to opt for a monthly standing order from your bank account for both gas and electricity. You can also choose the banker's order system for paying your telephone bill. Standing orders do not necessarily have to be monthly. They can correspond to normal times of payment: you pay the bill in one lump sum. You can have a copy of each bill sent to you in Britain so that you can check your bank statement to see if there are no errors. In any case it can be very useful to have a bank account in France, with a bank capable of administering your affairs in your absence.

Electric Central Heating

This system is well adapted to private houses: the equipment is light and easy to install. However, it requires efficient thermal insulation and a permanently controlled system of ventilation. If these conditions are adhered to, the complete installation comes under the label of integral electric heating. It is regulated by automatic and manual thermostats.

Although, for a long time, it was considered a luxury, electric heating is becoming a very interesting proposition in France, especially since the development of nuclear power. Today France supplies several neighbouring countries with electricity and even the British government considers that it could prove a useful way of obtaining cheap electricity without the danger of political controversy that new nuclear power stations in Britain would provoke! It is after all a practical, easy-to-control and pollution-free form of heating. It is certainly an option worth examining if you have a house that you only live in for a few months a year.

Solar Heating

The advantages of the so-called 'new' forms of energy (which are really based on principles as old as the hills) are that they are available more or less everywhere, are plentiful and are often free. On top of this, they are virtually pollution free. The disadvantages are that they often take up a lot of space, can only be used as background heating and cannot be relied upon at all times.

Solar heating in particular has quite a low output. It all depends, obviously, on where your house is situated. The principle is simply that it behaves like a greenhouse. Panels made from materials which absorb maximum heat (glass and plastic) are exposed to the sun. Piping is incorporated into these panels; heat is transmitted to the liquid flowing through the pipes and this circulates through the heating ducts. The public authorities favour this system a lot as it helps towards energy saving, and they encourage it by giving grants, in particular for the installation of water-heaters.

Solar panels can be of several types:

- a solar screen fitted to the roof of the house
- a solar screen fitted to the roof of a garage or workshop attached to the house (provided that the direction is right)

- an air-conditioned 'greenhouse' (sunroom). This works like a conservatory and can be used as a living room. Equally, it functions as a heat regulator and warm air reservoir. It is attached to a sunny wall of the house and openings situated high up provide ventilation. A system of moveable shutters controls the air flow between the sunroom and the house
- a 'Trombe wall', named after the engineer who invented it: this consists of a glass partition placed against a sun-drenched outside wall. The latter contains ventilation shafts which allow the heated air, circulating between glass and stone, into the house. Since hot air rises, it enters the house by the upper vent, causing the cooler air to pass out of the lower vent, become trapped between the two walls, and then heat up on contact with the glass and the sun's rays. An external isolating shutter can come down over the glass wall to prevent it from becoming too hot or to prevent the hot air from leaving the house at night.

The Heat Pump

This functions on roughly the same principle as a refrigerator. The refrigerator uses the 'cryogenic' properties of a liquid which, as it changes into a gas, gives off cold. In order to maintain a continuous cycle, the pump works without stopping, circulating a fluid which makes the liquid change into gas, then back into liquid and so on. The heat pump, by contrast, takes in air from outside, 'extracts' the heat and throws it out into the house. Like the solar system, this is a form of background heating only.

HUMIDITY

Coming from a country like Britain, where the last thing you want is more humidity, you will perhaps notice the passion the French have for humidifiers. In most of the country the climate is less humid than in Britain and in a well-heated house the air can quickly dry out.

The classic and traditional solution is to have little containers hanging from the radiators; these can also be found in some shops in Britain. They are often made of porcelain and very prettily decorated. There are also much more sophisticated (and more expensive!) types which work on batteries or electricity and diffuse a very fine water vapour into the room.

VENTILATION

Whether it is dry or humid the air must circulate without causing unplaughts. The ventilation of buildings is subject to a specific decree, that of March 24th 1982. This decree states that the ventilation system must be installed in all main rooms, by vents in outside walls, natural ducting or mechanical devices. It must also include air outlets in the utility areas, at least in the kitchen, the bathroom and W.C. A room which serves for both living and utility (for example a one-room flat with kitchen area) must have both inlets and outlets for air.

If there is a wall-mounted boiler in the kitchen the extraction of burned gases is subject to very precise rulings covering the diameter of the flue and the position of the air intake. For details you must refer to the decree of August 2nd 1977 regarding gas installations.

ELECTRICITY

The electricity supply is normally the responsibility of Electricity Of France (EDF), although sometimes it comes under the town's jurisdiction. You will find information and brochures about electrical equipment for houses in the Council Offices and the EDF information centres.

Electricity is distributed in either of two ways:

- by a single-phased current of 220 volts (in some villages the current is still only 110 volts but this is becoming less and less frequent)
- by a three-phased current of 380 volts

The power of appliances is measured in Watts, that of the installation in kilowatts. Consumption is measured in kilowatt/hours.

Tariffs

The EDF provides a choice of four rates according to the size of the electrical installation. They include a fixed tax which corresponds to charges set by the EDF and a variable tax based on the consumption of the user. The four rates are the same all over France, but you can choose the most economical according to the power of your electrical installation.

In all cases, the charges are subject to VAT (standard rate: 18.6 per cent).

You can choose between two different tariffs:

- Normal Tariff – there is no distinction between the times of consumption. The meter has only one dial.
- Night Tariff (*heures creuses*) – you have a discount for electricity used between 11.00 at night and 6.00 in the morning. The meter will have two dials. The rate is more expensive but the night tariff is useful when your consumption mainly comes from appliances which can function during the night, like water heating and central heating.

Out of the four rates offered, three do not include electric heating:

- Domestic Rate (*ménage*) – covers lighting and household appliances of low wattage (e.g. irons, refrigerators). Power: 3kW.
- Modern Convenience Rate (*confort*) – covers lighting, small domestic appliances plus one large appliance (e.g. washing machine, dishwasher, cooker). Power: 6kW.
- Delux Convenience Rate (*grand confort*) – allows, in addition to lighting and normal appliances, simultaneous use of two large appliances. Power: 9kW.

The fourth rate which includes electric heating is usually provided with a three-phase current of 220/380 volts. Power can be between 12 and 36kW.

E.D.F. also offers a "seasonal" rate system, by which the consumer pays a rather low tariff all the year round EXCEPT during a limited amount of days (around 30), spread over the winter months. E.D.F. warns him beforehand that from such a date to such a date, he will be paying maximum tariff. It is then up to the consumer to keep a vigilant eye on his electricity consumption, for instance by limiting the use of his more powerful appliances during that specific time. These "maximum tariff" days are meant to coincide with the colder winter periods, when E.D.F. is working at full capacity.

Connection to the Supply

When you move into a house which has just been wired or rewired, you need to be aware that the distributor (usually EDF) can only connect the supply when they have seen a 'certificate of conformity to regulations' (*attestation de conformité*) by the builder or electrician. This must be stamped by the Electricity Users National Safety Committee (*Comité National pour la Sécurité des Usagers de l'Electricité – CONSUEL*).

In practice, three weeks before you want to be connected, the installation firm must fill in this certificate and get it stamped by the local CONSUEL office. The electrician is then subject to a control check to see that the installation conforms to safety requirements. As far as connection charges are concerned, it all depends on whether there was a previous electrical supply in your house or not. If you have had a house built and need a completely new system linked up to the general network, the minimum price is around 2,500 francs for an above-ground connection, and 3,500 to 4,000 francs for an underground connection. If on the other hand, you need only to reconnect to an existing system, the connection will cost you about 100 francs.

Legal Requirements

The statutory rules concerning the use of electrical equipment and its implementation are governed by a legal standard known by the abbreviation NFC 15 100. Its application is now law in blocks of flats, as a result of the law of October 22nd 1969.

Sockets

They are 2-pin in living rooms; but, in kitchens, bathrooms and other rooms where there is damp or a conducting floor (tiling, cement etc.) the sockets must also have an earth pin linked to an earth connection. In bathrooms, switches and sockets must be out of reach of anyone in the bath or shower. However, it is not illegal, as in Britain, to have sockets there other than an electric razor socket. As for the switch, you may not persuade the electrician to replace it by a cord but you can at least ask him to install it outside the bathroom door.

WATER

Depending on where you are going to live, water will be distributed to you in one of the two following ways:

1. **The Collective Network Supply**. The town supplies water under pressure through underground pipes which run along public highways. From there, a system of pipes brings the water to the boundary of your property or to the meter when it is installed inside the building.

You, the user, must contribute towards the cost of connection. This allows you to decide the diameter of the piping up to your house, depending on what rate of flow you want. If you are going to use a lot of water (for instance to water the garden or fill a swimming pool), you will need a larger diameter than the standard one. On the other hand, the pressure of the water will depend on the town supply. If you find that the pressure is too low, it is always possible for you to install your own pump.

As for the connection charge, this depends on so many variable factors (distance from the town's network, depth of trenches, difficulty of digging the ground etc.) that it is impossible to put an exact price on it: it can range from 5,000 to 20,000 francs or even more. In any case, if you fall in love with a pretty little house deep in the country with no running water, it is imperative that you check on the price you will have to pay for a water supply. It's the kind of little joke that can double the price of the property!

2. **Private Water Supply**. Many houses in the country are not connected to the town water main. Water comes from nearby springs or from a well. You must check very carefully that the water is drinkable. Only the local office of supply (*Direction Départementale de l'Equipement*) can give you the go-ahead to use this water, after laboratory tests.

These laboratory tests will also provide information as to whether or not your water is hard. It may be that you will need a water softener. Several areas of France have hard water, particularly Charente-Maritime, Picardy, Périgord, Haute Savoie, South Jura and Champagne.

Whatever your system of water supply, there is one item that you will not find in French houses: the tank in the roof. All the water in the house comes from the same source, whatever type that is. So there is no difference between the water in the bathroom and in the kitchen.

Hot Water

Where water is concerned, you have a choice between several types of heating. You can have instant hot water tanks to different water and bath-heaters.

The kitchen water-heater is capable of producing 5 litres of water a minute at 40°c or 2.5 litres a minute at 65°c. It can only be used to supply one tap.

The bath water-heater, depending on its size, can be used either to supply several taps, provided they are not all used at the same time or to supply vast quantities of water simultaneously and feed all the sanitary equipment in the house. Finally some very powerful water-heaters suit large families.

You could also install an immersion-heater of the type which is to be found almost everywhere in Britain – with the difference that the storage unit is usually hung on the bathroom wall, not installed in a linen cupboard.

There is also a mixed system: the tank supplies hot water as long as it stays at a certain temperature, generally around 40°c. As soon as the temperature drops, the boiler supplies hot water direct, but at a slower rate.

Fittings

Kitchen and bathroom fittings differ very little from those in Britain. Obviously you will find, in France more bathrooms with a bidet; on this subject, if the bathroom is small, you can easily find bidets which are mounted on a wheeled support, allowing them to be slid under a washbasin or into a cupboard.

If your kitchen is not very big, why not think of having a dishwasher with a hob on top of it? There are various makes available.

Drainage

This is a question that you will have to go into without delay if you are buying, restoring or building a detached house. In some places you have the benefit of a common purification and sewerage network. This is called mains drainage (*le tout à l'égout*). However, it often happens in country places that this network does not exist, so you will have to install a septic tank if there is not one there already. You will find yourself up against one of the five following situations:

1. There is **split mains drainage**. That means that there are two networks of pipes, one which takes away rainwater, the other which evacuates effluent. In this case, all you have to do is to pay the connection to the sewer. It's possible that this type of sewer does not exist yet but is planned for by the town, sometime in the future. You too ought to plan for pipes likely to be connected to this sytem.

2. There is **single mains drainage**. Rainwater and effluent are collected together. You will have a peephole (*un regard*) installed, which is in fact a small manhole, so that you can check that the water is flowing away properly and if necessary, have the pipes cleaned out.

3. There is only **a rainwater sewer**. This means that only rainwater is collected. However, you may possibly be allowed to be connected to this network to take away sluice water (from the WC), which will first need to pass through a septic tank and then a purification plant, and domestic waste water (from the kitchen and bathroom) which should first pass through a degreasing plant. Rainwater will be fed directly into the water system.

4. There is only **an effluent sewer**. This happens quite often in rural areas; it will mean that rainwater is simply channeled towards a ditch.

5. There is **no mains drainage** whatsoever; then you have to install your own system. The classic answer is the septic tank, containing a degreasing device and an absorption plate; if you buy a house with this system installed, do not forget to find out how many times a year you will need to have it cleaned out. A more

modern solution is a micro-purification plant. This consists of a mechanical system which speeds up the 'digestion' of the effluent by bacteria (as in the septic tank) by constantly agitating the contents of the underground trough.

THE TELEPHONE

After having often been criticized for its lack of sophistication the French telephone system is, today, one of the most modern of all European networks.

Codes

Since October 1985, French telephone numbers have consisted of eight digits. As a general rule, the regional telephone codes are now permanently part of these digits. In practice, this means that if you are in Nantes, for example, and you want to call someone in the same town, you have to dial 40 in front of the number, whereas, in the past, these two digits were only dialled if you were calling from outside the code area.

For Paris, whose numbers already had seven digits, a 4 has been added to the beginning of each one. Take care though; this does not mean that you no longer have to dial the 1 before the number you are calling if you are phoning from outside the city. To call a number in another county (*département*) you no longer have to dial the 16 (which corresponds to the 0 of the English telephone system); you simply dial the number required. One exception: Paris, which you reach from the provinces by dialling 16, followed by a tone, then 1 and finally the required number. In the same way, if you are calling the provinces from Paris you must dial 16 – tone – the required number.

To phone abroad from France, nothing has changed. You dial 19 – wait for the tone – dial the code of the country – and then the required number (NB when calling a number in Britain do not forget to omit the 0 before the regional code, or you will never get through). To go through to the international operator you dial 19 – wait for the tone – then 33 followed by the number of the national code for the country (44 for Britain) and the operator will answer.

Installation

If you install a telephone line in your house, you must make your application to the Post Office authorities (PTT: *Postes-Télégraphes, Téléphones*). The local post office will give you the details. If you call in a private installer, they will take care of the red tape.

What is important, is to go ahead in plenty of time. Delays in installation are not too bad, on average, but it all depends, obviously on where your house is situated. In an area that is well supplied, it will probably only take a few days. In more isolated areas you may have to wait some weeks, if not months. Whatever the case, it is in your interest, to avoid further expense, to have trenches for telephone wires dug at the same time as the other work on the house. Otherwise you can ask for a connection above ground with a wire going from the house to the pylon, but it is unsightly.

If you only have one telephone point in the house, the PTT insist that it be put in the living room. In general, the ruling demands that telephone points be positioned more than 20cm from any corner of the room, and 5cm at least from the ground, if they are fixed to the skirting board, or 15cm up if there is no skirting board.

Charges

If you are having a new line installed, the connection charge is 250 francs. If the line is already in existence, it costs 50 francs. The rental charge is 39 francs a month.

Regarding the charges for calls, these are all printed in the telephone directory. As in Britain, there are certain times of day when the tariffs are reduced:

from 10.30 p.m. to 06.00 a.m., the reduction is 65 per cent

from 06.00 a.m. to 08.00 a.m. and from 9.30 p.m. to 10.30 p.m., the reduction is 50 per cent

from 12.30 p.m. to 1.30 p.m. and from 6.00 p.m. to 9.30 p.m. the reduction is 30 per cent

The peak time (*heures rouges*), full tariff goes from 08.00 a.m. to 12.30 p.m. and from 1.30 p.m. to 6.00 p.m.

Minitel

Several million French people are now connected to Minitel, which is a computer-based information system linked by telephone.

With Minitel you can, for a start, obtain all the information in the telephone directories. You can also obtain a whole list of other information, ranging from the state of your bank account to the timetables of aircraft from such and such an airport to such and such a destination; you can even get BBC Ceefax if you want the daily news in Britain.

Minitel is basically the equivalent of Prestel, but it is designed for the general public and not just for the business world. It has also become a means of communication between subscribers, who communicate through the Minitel link, a bit like CB enthusiasts or radio amateurs.

It will cost a basic rate of 61 francs 60 an hour. As for the equipment, this is rented from the PTT. Price: currently 85 francs a month.

TELEVISION

If you intend installing a television, your first worry will be about reception. You will obviously not get good reception if your house is at the bottom of a valley or if you are surrounded by blocks of flats. Your neighbours will be able to give you all the necessary points of information, otherwise you will have to ask the advice of an installer.

Cable TV

To receive the main French TV channels, one single aerial is sufficient. Some housing developments are equipped with cable television. Each house is linked by cable to a collective aerial; individual aerials are not allowed. A very strict ruling governs the quality of reception. This has a certain aesthetic advantage, as it avoids a forest of aerials which does nothing for the urban landscape.

A certain number of localities – or districts of large towns – have their own cable TV available. If you think that programmes put out by this system will interest you, you would be wise to think ahead about installing cable for the eventual link-up when it becomes available.

Satellite TV

Satellite TV is still not very developed. The individuals better able to benefit from it are those who are in a cable TV area, because there may already be a satellite dish in the locality which redistributes pictures received by satellite.

Obviously you find individual dishes but they are very expensive and it is not at all certain you will find a specialist capable of installing it correctly.

For traditional TV the annual tax is 560 francs for a colour set. The tax on video recorders has been withdrawn.

THE GARDEN

Giving advice on gardening to British readers is rather like teaching your grandmother to suck eggs. In all humility, we will confine ourselves to some basic points where from you will surely work miracles.

Climate

The climate is obviously an essential element. In general, France is considered to have a temperate climate but within this definition there are variations.

The Oceanic Climate

This stretches from the plains bordering the Atlantic to the coastal areas of the North Sea, passing through Brittany and the Channel coast (where the wind is the greatest enemy in the garden). It is a humid climate, especially in Brittany and maritime Flanders. The temperature is rather mild, winters are lenient and summers not too hot. Brittany is a paradise for hydrangeas and camelias. In Flanders the soil is sandy and exposed to sea winds and to a salt-charged humidity.

The Continental Climate

You find this in the Ardennes, in Alsace, Lorraine and in the Upper Saône Valley. Summers are hot and winters are harsh with quite short intermediate seasons.

The Mild Oceanic Climate

This is an intermediate climate, somewhere between the previous two, which allows all kinds of things to be grown. It stretches through Artois, Champagne, the Ile de France, the Pays de La Loire, Limousin and Languedoc Toulousain.

The Mediterranean Climate

This stretches along the Mediterranean coast, covers the Lower Rhône Valley and Corsica. The temperatures are relatively warm in winter and quite high in summer. It rains very little from June to September. Winds like the Mistral and the Tramontane are very dry – thus playing a harmful rôle in spreading forest fires. However, when you have a supply of water available, you can work wonders in the garden. Orange trees flower from Cannes to Menton, as well as palm trees and mimosa.

The Mountain Climate

This provides an infinite variety of micro-climates. The annual period of vegetation is shorter than on the plain and the choice of plants that can be grown more limited. Depending on the altitude and shelter, you can find delphiniums, lupins, phlox, alpine plants, heather and rock conifers.

Whatever kind of vegetation you intend planting, it is very important to know that you are not allowed to take into France any trees, bushes, flowers or plants without a 'health licence' – from the country of origin of the plant concerned – which is rather complicated and expensive to obtain.

For a long time, the French garden was invisible, surrounded by high walls or fences. This is beginning to change a little, especially on modern housing estates where fences are often positively forbidden.

However, even if they want to withdraw behind their walls, the French have to keep to a number of laws.

Rules and Regulations

If they want to install any kind of building in the garden (garage, summerhouse etc.) which has a greater surface area than 2.50 sq.m with a ceiling of more than 1.80 m. they need to obtain a building permit. They also need to respect constraints, if there are any, governing rights of way, fences, openings etc.

If a party wall straddles the boundary of the property, the two owners must be in agreement, before any work is done on it as it implies a sharing of building, maintenance and repair costs, proportional to the rights of each owner. The height of a wall separating adjoining properties is limited to 2.6m maximum in a town of fewer than 50,000 inhabitants and 3.2m in a larger town. If the land is not on the same level on either side of the wall, the height is measured from the higher level of land.

If you plant a hedge, the minimum distance between the centre of the hedge and the line separating the properties must be 0.5m for a height of less than 2m, and 2m if the bushes are higher. The minimum distance in relation to the public highway is 1m.

Obviously you cannot make an opening in a party wall without your neighbour's consent. You can build a path inside your garden without having to keep to any rules and regulations, as this concerns a private way but you must consult the local department of supply to find out if you have the right to link your path to the public highway and to have what the French call a 'boat' (*un bateau*), a lowering of the pavement to make access easier for vehicles.

You do not have to obtain a building permit for a swimming pool completely or half-set into the ground (a) if the surface area of the water is less than 100 sq.m and the visible height is not more than 60cm; or (b) if you do not have to erect a shelter, a supporting wall or a party wall. It is, however, essential that you obtain a copy of the rules on construction techniques from the *Chambre Syndicale des Industries de la Piscine* (Employers' Federation of Swimming Pool Industries) and get the work carried out by professionals. These should be duly qualified by the *Organisme Professionnel de Qualification et de Classification du Bâtiment* (OPQCR – Professional Organization for the Quality and Classification of Buildings) or even by the *Organisme Professionel de Qualification des Réalisations Sports et Loisirs* (OPQRSL – Professional Organization for the Quality of Sport and Leisure Creations).

The Employer's Federation of Swimming Pool Industries will give you all the necessary details concerning insurance – you do not have to insure a swimming pool like a house; on the other hand the builder must give you a 10-year guarantee covered by an insurance certificate.

Finally, respecting the local environment and the architecture is a must if you want to keep the authorities off your back.

In short...

- The installing and repair of electrical and plumbing facilities, heating, etc. is subject to precise and stringent laws and regulations: you cannot improvise. Learn what they are before starting any do-it-yourself.

- There are tax deductions for insulating your home provided it is your main residence.

- No tree, flower or plant can be brought into France without a special licence.

USEFUL ADDRESSES

Agence Nationale pour
l'Amélioration de l'Habitat
(ANAH)
17 Rue de la Paix
75002 Paris
Tel: 42 61 57 23

Association Confort Régulation
BP 458
75830 Paris Cedex 17
Tel: 43 29 38 85

Comit Professionnel du Butane
et du Propane
4 Avenue Hoche
75008 Paris
Tel: 47 66 77 20

Promotélec (electricity control)
and CONSUEL
52 Boulevard Malesherbes
75008 Paris
Tel: 45 22 87 70

Comit Professionnel du Pétrole
51 Boulevard de Courcelles
75008 Paris
Tel: 47 66 03 82

Chambre Syndicale des
Industries de la Piscine
22 Rue du Général Foy
75008 Paris
(Swimming pools)

Fédération des Fabricants de Tuiles et de Briques de France
17 Rue Letellier
75015 Paris
Tel: 45 78 65 00
(Roof tiles) ·

Consumer Protection

Institut National de la
Consommation (INC)
80 Rue Lecourbe
75015 Paris
Tel: 45 67 35 58

Union Fédérale des
Consommateurs que Choisir
11 Rue Guènot
75011 Paris
Tel: 43 48 55 48

10
DAILY PRACTICALITIES

THE RIGHT OF RESIDENCY – REMOVAL

Obviously the measures described here concern those of you who are going to settle in France either for several years or permanently. If you are going there on holiday or on business, these do not apply to you, *unless* your stay exceeds three months without a break.

(a) If you are going to live in France for a period, one of the first steps you must take will be in Britain. You must visit the French Consulate which deals with the area of your place of residence (see list at end of chapter) to obtain a certificate of change of residence (*Certificat de Changement de Résidence*). In addition, before leaving, you must assemble a number of documents which you will have to produce at the consulate:

- two photocopies of your passport.
- evidence of your residence in Britain. This should consist of a declaration made by a British local authority, such as a Mayor, Registrar of Rolls, Justice of the Peace or solicitor. It should specify your nationality, your address in Britain and the length of time you have resided at this address. If you cannot obtain this statement, you can write a personal declaration and have it witnessed by a Commissioner for Oaths. If you are already in France, this declaration should be made in the presence of a British Consul.
- two copies of a detailed inventory *in French* of personal articles you wish to take to France (stating the value of the more expensive items). These inventories should be dated and signed, and accompanied by a handwritten declaration stating that valuable items have been in your property for more than

three months (six months for mobile homes, private vehicles, private aeroplanes and pleasure boats), that they are destined for private use and will *not* be disposed of in France within a period of twelve months from the date of entry. (For a copy of this declaration in French, see the end of the chapter.) For valuable objects, French Customs will issue a special form, entitled CERFA 301584, at the time of importation.

You will be requested to pay a Consular fee, which amounts to a maximum of £3.30.

(b) If you intend to settle definitely in France, you must obtain a Permanent Residence Visa (*Visa d'Etablissement*). You should apply for the relevant forms at the Visa Section of the French Consulate in London (address at the end of the chapter) at least *eight weeks* before you leave Britain. The Consulate will require six or seven identity photographs – standard passport size – as well as your passport. If you are going to work in France, you should also provide a copy of your work contract, or of your lease of business premises, in short any document proving that you will have a job there.

If you are not going to have a professional occupation, because you are a pensioner or a student, you will have to present:

- a letter from your bank stating what capital you possess and what your yearly income is, or
- a 'certificate of lodging' (*certificat d'hébergement*) signed by a person in France who undertakes to provide for you. This document should be countersigned by the local Chief Inspector of Police (*Commissaire*) or the Mayor (*Maire*). You must personally endorse the certificate as follows: *Le bénéficiaire du présent certificat d'hébergement approuve et accepte expressément les termes de l'engagement souscrit par M. ou Mme X...*
- an affidavit drawn up and stamped in the presence of a Commissioner for Oaths, stating whether or not you have been convicted for a criminal offence of any kind, or even been made bankrupt, in Britain or elsewhere.

  The letter from the bank and the affidavit should be accompanied by two copies of the texts translated into French.
- a health certificate drawn up by one of the doctors accredited by the French Consulate.

At the same time as you contact the Consulate, you must obtain permission from Customs to transfer your furniture and personal possessions. You must send three copies of your inventory plus a form obtained from the Consulate to the General Customs Office (*Direction Générale des Douanes*) nearest to your future residence (address provided by the Consulate) or else to a Customs agent, if you intend to use one. If you do, your removal company will be able to give you the name of the agent they usually deal with. Together with the documents for Customs, enclose proof of your residence in France – for instance a copy of the contract you signed when buying or renting your home in France.

You won't have to pay duty or VAT on your furniture and domestic goods, provided they have been in your possession for more than six months. Obviously, if you want to take over new sheets or new curtains for your future home, nobody is going to make a fuss unless the quantity is so enormous it becomes suspect! It's up to you, anyway, to work out if it's worth paying for the transport of new furnishings when you have just as good a chance of finding the same in France – from Habitat to Sandersons by way of Laura Ashley.

So much for red tape; you will also have to take care of the practicalities, like looking for a trustworthy removal firm. The French Consulate and the French Embassy can provide a list of removal companies well acquainted with the subtleties of moving between Britain and France. The removers will help you make sure that you have all the necessary documents; in fact, they will need copies of some of these documents, like the inventory and Certificate or Visa of Residence. Obviously, you will be well advised to shop around and ask for estimates from different companies. In any case, there is no escaping the fact that the average cost of moving between Britain and France amounts to several thousand pounds, especially if you add 'details' like the insurance covering the whole operation or the VAT on transport that you will have to pay in France...

Theoretically, your removal should be completed in one go. If that's not possible, on your first passage through Customs, you must provide a complete inventory, specifying when the following trips are due. You will have to go through the same Customs port each time and complete the whole move within *12 months* of your official change of residence.

Once you are in France, try to register as soon as possible at your nearest British Consulate (see the addresses at the end of the chapter). It isn't compulsory for a British citizen, but you would be well inspired to do so, if only because the Consulate can provide you with useful information such as: where to find doctors, lawyers, translators, places of worship, schools, etc; whether or not you can vote in your own country; as well as explaining all the legal and administrative formalities you must see to, now you are in France.

For instance, you will have to ask for a Residence Permit as soon as you have settled into your new home. If you live in a large town or in the *chef-lieu de département*, which is the equivalent of a county capital, you go to the *Préfecture*; if you live in a smaller locality, you go to the council offices at the Town Hall (*Mairie*), where your request will be transmitted to the relevant *Préfecture*. You will have to provide a proof of identification (in your case, your passport), four identity photographs and your Change of Residence Certificate or Permanent Establishment Visa from the French Consulate in Britain. Do not forget your Permit or Visa, otherwise the local authorities will make you repeat the whole procedure you went through in Britain.

Once these formalities are done with, you will be issued with a Residence Card (*Carte de Séjour*), valid for 12 months, which will not cost you anything. Two months before this residence period expires, you must ask for a renewal, which will be valid for three years. You will be asked for written proof (e.g. work contract, bank statement) that you have financial support. At the end of the three years, you will be issued with a Residence Permit valid for 10 years.

Remember that, in France, you should always carry some form of identification, plus, as a foreigner, your Residence Permit. Whatever certain foreign newspapers may say, you definitely do not get stopped by truncheon-wielding policemen at every street corner; however, should you be involved in a car accident or a bomb alert (which is, unfortunately, a possibility in our countries these days), you run the risk of ending up at the nearest police station if you can't show proof of identity. It must be stressed that the same treatment would be meted out to a French citizen.

Finally, before leaving Britain, make sure you have sorted out your financial and fiscal affairs with the relevant authorities. If you still have interests in Britain – property, bonds, shares, etc – your accountant and your solicitor should be able to advise you on the best way of making your investments yield a profit without your being snowed under by taxes or having to become a tax exile. If you want to know, before leaving Britain, what your individual tax situation will be in France, there are several tax consultants, specialising in French and British tax legislation, available through the Franco–British Chamber of Commerce in London.

TAKING YOUR ANIMALS

You can bring your domestic animals with you to France, provided they are at least three months old. The fact that rabies exists on the Continent does not mean that you have to go in constant fear for the life of your pets. Rabies affects mostly wild animals, like foxes; nevertheless, this does not absolve you from observing certain rather strict rules.

If you want to bring your pet onto French territory, you must obtain, for the benefit of Customs, an anti-rabies certificate (*certificat contre la rage*) signed by a British vet registered with the Ministry of Agriculture, Fisheries and Food, or else a health certificate (*certificat de bonne santé*) issued *five days* at the earliest before departure by a vet registered at the Ministry of Agriculture, Fisheries and Food. If you can obtain neither of these, for want of a registered vet in your neighbourhood, you can ask for a certificate from the Ministry itself, stating that Britain has been rabies-free for more than three years and that your pet has been living on British territory for more than six months or, if it is younger, from the moment of its birth. There again, this certificate must be issued five days at the earliest before departure.

But, if you can manage to have the animal vaccinated against rabies and obtain the relevant vaccination certificate, it really would be the best option, because it would avoid your having to rush to the vet's the minute you get to France, where rabies vaccination is compulsory. Your pet must be vaccinated less than a year before you leave for France; otherwise it will have to go for a booster dose. Dogs must also be vaccinated against hardpad and distemper, cats against typhus and feline gastro-enteritis.

Having taken all these precautions, you may then find, to your annoyance, that French Customs officers will hardly glance at your precious certificates. Never mind: if they don't get checked on arrival, you may well be stopped further inland by the 'flying customs' (*la Douane volante* or, more familiarly, *la Volante*), i.e. Customs officers driving around in cars, who have the right to stop you anywhere in France. In any case, you will, eventually, have to show these papers to a French vet. Because rabies shots are compulsory, every dog that has been vaccinated must have the identification number of that particular dose tatooed on the inside of one of its ears.

A word of advice: whatever you do, it would be most unwise to count on the Customs officers' apparent lack of interest to try and get your pet into France without the appropriate papers. If, on the very day you cross over, Customs have decided to crack down on careless animal owners, your dog, cat, hampster or pet rat will immediately be packed off back to Britain. Once there, the situation is, unfortunately, all too clear: the animal is immediately put into quarantine, at your expense, and you will be very lucky if you manage to avoid paying a hefty fine.

Please note: you cannot take more than three domestic animals at a time into France.

A final piece of advice: if you don't want to pay fines of several hundred francs, do not forget that, in French parks, dogs must be kept on a lead. The appropriate warnings are usually posted up in parks; if you don't see any, don't take that as meaning that your dog can roam free. It may simply be that the boards have been vandalized or are stuck in some rather unobvious place. These restrictions do not apply to very big parks like the Bois de Boulogne or the Bois de Vincennes in Paris; nevertheless, even there, you will find a few no-go zones, so make sure you are actually walking your dog in an obviously unrestricted area.

CARS AND DRIVING REGULATIONS

If, as a future resident in France, you wish to take your own car over, you will have to pay French VAT and road tax (*vignette*). Knowing this, you may find it worth your while to buy a new car before leaving Britain because, if you observe the necessary rules, you can avoid paying British VAT and road tax.

The first rule is that your car must be bought less than six months before you leave.

Secondly, when you apply to the French Consulate for all your residency documents, ask for a vehicle import certificate (*déclaration d'importation de véhicule*). The car must go through Customs at the same time as the rest of your belongings, and you must be there, with all the documents relating to the vehicle. If you do not have a removal van going over to France (because, for instance, you are renting furnished lodgings), you can take the car over on its own, provided, yet again, you, the owner, are present, complete with documents – including the import certificate.

At the time of buying the car, you must be able to prove that you are going to live abroad for more than a year. Beware: you cannot buy the car just anywhere; only the manufacturers or sole agents of a particular make are allowed to sell tax-free. As for your insurance, it has to take into account the total value of the car, including the taxes you did not pay, for the period you are still in Britain.

You will be allowed to drive the car in Britain only during the six months preceding your departure. If this is delayed, it might be a good idea to take the car abroad anyway and, if possible, leave it with a person – or a garage – you can trust until you arrive. If you don't, you will have to pay British road tax and VAT, otherwise you would be committing an offence.

When passing through French Customs, you will be asked for proof of your residence in France, the registration documents of the car, as well as a signed statement from the vendor saying that you have not paid road tax or VAT. They will then forward to your new home a Customs certificate (*certificat de Douane*). Once you have this customs certificate, take it, together with the other car documents and your passport, to the nearest agent for that particular make. He will tell you if your car complies with French road regulations as well as technical specifications (e.g. yellow headlights), so that it can take the road test; he will also help you obtain your French registration document (*carte grise*) – without it, you cannot hope to take your car onto a French road.

NB: You are not allowed to sell your car during the six months following receipt of the *carte grise*.

At the same time, remember to take out some car insurance. Only when these steps have been taken can you have French number plates fitted to your car, at the end of the six months during which you are allowed 'TT' (tax-free) plates. TT stands for *transit temporaire* or temporary transit. When you get French number plates, you will then have to pay road tax and VAT (in France, VAT on cars is 28 per cent, but you will be charged on the value of a six-months old car, not a new one). You will have two stickers, one for the road tax, one for the insurance, which must be applied to the *top right-hand* corner of your windscreen.

If you move from one county (*département*) to another you have to change your plates and registration document. Cars are in fact registered within the county and they carry the number of that county (75 for Paris, 13 for the Bôuches du Rhône, 30 for the Gard, 60 for the Oise, 06 for the Alpes-Maritimes, etc.).

Your Driving Licence

As regards your British driving licence, this is valid in France for 12 months after you have obtained your residence permit. Before this period is up, you must exchange your licence for a French one. To do this, you must go to the nearest *Préfecture* (in Paris, go to the *Préfecture de Police*) taking your certificate of change of residence or your *visa d'établissement*. Your original driving licence will be returned to the appropriate British authorities. Being a national of the Common Market, you do not have to take another driving test in France.

Traffic Rules and Customs

Nevertheless, it is in your own interest to obtain a copy of the French highway code and, if you do not have too many problems with the language, to go through it, as there are differences in road-signs and rules. To take just one example, French drivers must observe the *priorité à droite*: (give way to traffic from the right) at junctions, unless the road signs show otherwise. If the road on which you are driving carries a yellow lozenge-shaped sign, *you* have right of way.

Radar traps

It is also interesting to know that in France, the police have the right to install concealed radars to trap motorists who exceed the speed limit. As a general rule, they do at least put up signs to warn you that you are passing through a radar-controlled zone, because the idea is to prevent excess speed, especially in built-up areas, rather than to set upon careless drivers once they have committed the offence. You will no doubt discover quite soon that in France you can obtain little 'bleeper' gadgets for your car which warn you that there is a radar close by. They are illegal! If you do come across them on sale or being advertised, we leave you to draw your own conclusions as to the French sense of discipline!

Headlight-flashing

Failing the electronic signal, you will notice that sometimes cars coming towards you will flash their headlights. If several cars join in this little game, it is not that you are driving oddly but that there is either a radar trap or a police car parked a little further on, watching the traffic. It should be noted that this habit is also illegal... although this does not stop it happening. It is starting to be practised in Britain too.

On the subject of headlights, if you want to avoid a terrible accident, do not forget that in France, when motorists flash their lights at you, it does not mean that they are letting you pass. They are in fact warning you that they are about to overtake or cross in front of you. This is the normal function of headlights, according to the highway codes, including the British one. So, if someone flashes their lights at you at a crossroads, rather than taking it as a courteous gesture, beware of a collision, and slow down or stop to let the other pass.

Drinking and driving

The French police have the right to administer breath tests at random and if the result is positive, they can make you leave your car where it is and go on your way as best you can. The permitted limit of alcohol in the blood is 0.8 grams per litre. Driving while under the influence of alcohol can make you liable to a prison sentence (2 months to 2 years) and a fine (2,000 to 30,000 Francs) as well as to losing your licence for up to three years if you have up to 1.20 gm of alcohol per litre of blood. Above this level, a three-year suspension is automatic.

Speed limits

The speed limits on French roads are as follows:

- 130 km/h on motorways
- 110 km/h on dual carriageways
- 90 km/h on ordinary roads
- 60 km/h in built-up areas
- 45 km/h in towns

Diesel

Many French motorists drive cars which run on diesel. As France does not have its own oil, petrol costs quite a lot, certainly more than in Britain. Diesel-run cars are therefore more common in France and you will have no problem finding diesel pumps at service stations.

Finally, do not forget: there are tolls on French motorways.

HEALTH, SOCIAL SECURITY AND RETIREMENT

These are all points on which you should obtain as much information as you can *before* leaving Britain. Every person is an individual case and it is best that your file should be as clear and complete as possible before you start trying to explain your problems at a French social security office. It would be a good idea to ask for advice and information at the Overseas Branch of the DHSS (the
address is at the end of the chapter). You can obtain from them a whole series of brochures explaining the social security, child benefit and medical systems.

If you work in France you will be subject to the same social security procedures as the French and you will have the same benefits.

Arrangements are made for you under European Community Regulations. These regulations give equal treatment and protection of benefits rights to:

- employed and self-employed people who are or have been insured as such under the UK National Insurance Scheme
- National Insurance pensioners and other beneficiaries who have been employed or self-employed
- dependants and survivors of the above-mentioned

These regulations do not normally apply to non-employed people unless they pay voluntary insurance as non-employed or have at some time been insured as employed or self-employed.

The practical moves to make are the following: as soon as you are settled into your new home, look up the address of the social security office nearest to you (in the phone book, it will be under Sécurité Sociale or else C.P.A.M. which stands for Centre de Paiement de l'Assurance Maladie).

Ask your employer to sign an employment certificate (déclaration d'emploi) stating that you work for him and send it off to your social security office (it must be the one near your home NOT near your place of work), together with details of your date and place of birth.

You will then be issued with a social security card and number. The card also bears the "identification" number if the centre you must apply to if you want your medical expenses reimbursed.

In the case of a couple where only one is working, both are covered by the same social security card and number; this applies also to their children.

If you can afford it, you may find it useful to subscribe to a private medical insurance scheme in Britain, checking that it covers medical expenses abroad. Find out from your insurance company if your current insurance can be extended. Many medical insurance organizations are ready to change your national insurance into international insurance.

The DHSS will send you leaflet number SA 29. This will explain:

(a) family, maternity, sickness and unemployment benefits (paragraphs 21 to 24).
(b) provisions (para. 28).
(c) voluntary contributions to National Insurance (para. 11): it is possible in effect to become a voluntary contributor to the UK scheme, so as to maintain your UK record for pension purposes.
(d) state invalidity and retirement pension or widow's benefit: as soon as you reach the age which, in your country, gives you the right to retire, you must ask for Form No. E121 which confirms this right. If you show this form to your Social Security office in France you will be automatically entitled to

a French Social Security pension, even if you never actually contributed *in France*.

(e) Child Benefit: whether you can still receive Child Benefit after leaving Britain will depend on how long you intend to stay abroad.

If you, your child or both of you are going abroad temporarily, Child Benefit is payable for up to eight weeks. If you are going abroad for less than eight weeks, you do not need to tell your local Social Security officer or the Child Benefit centre. If you are going to France permanently, with your child or children, as a national of an EEC country, you may be able to get British Child Benefit if you are working for an employer in Britain or are getting a state retirement pension. Otherwise, if you are working for a French employer, you may be able to get *French* Child Benefit. For details on these specific arrangements, you must write to the Child Benefit Centre (address at the end of the chapter).

(f) pensions: if you are entitled to a UK retirement pension (including an age addition if you are 80 or over), or widow's pension, it can be paid to you from Britain, at the same rate, by means of payable orders sent at monthly or quarterly intervals, either directly to you in France or else to a bank account, building society or a person of your choosing in Britain.

If you are going to settle in France, whether to work or to retire, do *not* ask for the well-known form E111 as this specifically applies to those who are planning a short stay abroad. (Using the E111 certificate, they can get 70 to 80 per cent of costs refunded for: hospital treatment; dental treatment; other medical care; prescribed medicines. All the details about form E111 are contained in brochure SA30.)

Despite the bridges thrown across EEC countries to facilitate access to social security, the systems are far from identical. In France, visits to the doctor, drugs and medical care are not automatically free; you are reimbursed afterwards. Of course this is not the case when people are too poor to pay the money in advance, for example for a serious operation followed by weeks in hospital. In these cases the authorities take adequate measures.

When it comes to choosing your medical practitioner, it is very important to know if he has signed an agreement (une convention) with the Social Security Services. If he has, he is known as "conventionné" – in this case you will get your medical expenses reimbursed. If he isn't, then like in Britain, you pay the whole of the bill. This system also applies to clinics.

If you want to find a practitioner that is "conventionné", you can obtain the list of doctors practising near your home at your social security centre or by consulting the Minitel.

Should you require the services of a medical auxiliary (a nurse, a physiotherapist etc) you will only be reimbursed if you first obtain a prescription signed by your G.P. and stating your need. Who you then go to is left up to you.

Whereas, if you want to see a medical specialist (pediatrician, cardiologist, orthopedist...) you do not need to go through your G.P. to get your money back from social security.

You are not totally reimbursed: only 70 to 80 per cent of expenses. If you want the rest back you must subscribe to an individual insurance (*mutuelle*) – which is usually a matter of course for working people. In any case, to get your money back, you must definitely be registered with Social Security either through your employer or directly at a local office.

On the other hand, you are free to choose a doctor (GP or specialist) when and where you want. You are not required, on arrival, to register at a surgery and sign on with a doctor. This freedom of choice means a lot to the French and opinion polls show that they prefer, by a large majority, this system to a non-paying one without a free choice of consultant, GP, specialist or whoever. The same goes for dental care.

Another advantage that the French appreciate very much is the ease with which the doctor makes house-calls when you are ill.

If you give birth to children in France, you will be given a health book (*Carnet de Santé*) for each child. This is a small notebook in which every medical event in the child's life must be noted: vaccinations, childhood illnesses, medical care, operations etc.

When it comes to animals, vets are in general well qualified, which is not surprising in a country which boasts more dogs than Britain! It's a profession which is very popular with young people, but although there are many applicants, few are chosen, as the entrance examinations and studies at veterinary school have the reputation of being even more difficult than those at medical school!

INSURANCE

A great many of you will already be insured with a British company, if only for your house. The most logical step therefore, is to contact this company before you leave, and find out if they can equally well insure you in France. Most major British insurance companies have offices in France.

Life Insurance

For certain types of insurance, like life insurance which you may have taken out for the benefit of a close relative, there is nothing to prevent you keeping it up in Britain, as long as you continue to pay your subscriptions, either directly from an account with your bank in Britain or by bank transfer. In the event of your death, the insurance will be paid to the beneficiaries even if they, too, live in France.

House Insurance

If you rent or buy a home in France, you are going to have to subscribe to a housing insurance scheme. The law does not demand this, but if you rent, the owner has a perfect right to demand that you be insured and if you buy, you are hardly likely to obtain a loan without taking out insurance.

If you are renting: to help you decide what type of insurance you must take out, this is how the relationship between tenant and owner is governed according to the terms of the civil code. The tenant is:

- answerable for any damage or loss which occurs during his stay, unless he can prove that he was not to blame.
- answerable in case of fire unless he can prove that the fire happened by accident, by circumstances beyond his control or because of structural faults.
- responsible for damage and loss caused by other people living in the house or by sub-tenants.

Whether you are owner or tenant, you should take out an 'all risks' insurance (*assurance multirisques*) which covers risks of fire, theft, flood, storm or tempest, explosion, broken windows and damage by a third party (if they live with you). This insurance, however, does not cover accidents caused to others because of the house itself (e.g. a tile falling off the roof onto a passer-by). For this, you will need a separate insurance, as well as for damage to others caused by someone who does not usually live in your house or by an animal, and similarly for any accident which may happen to or be caused by your children at, or on the way to, school.

Naturally, if yours is a holiday home which lies empty for part of the year you can expect to pay rather high insurance premiums.

You will also need to check how far you are covered for theft with your 'all risks' policy. Do not trust the general conditions of the contract which list all the guarantees offered to the insured. You should check, in the specific conditions, the list of guarantees which *apply* to you and for which you have paid.

Take care: when you buy a property the notary is not responsible for arranging insurance. You must do this yourself or through your lawyer. If you take out French insurance, do not forget that your furniture, carpets and valuables will be estimated according to their value in France, not in Britain.

Making a Claim

To make an insurance claim, you need to inform your insurer within five days of the incident (24 hours in the case of theft). You must give them: the number of the policy, the date and nature of the incident, a description of the damage plus the estimated value of the damaged or stolen goods.

Car Insurance

In general, car insurance is quite expensive in France by comparison with Britain, especially in large towns. The difference is accounted for mainly by the absence of a 'no fault' policy – in other words you must insure yourself specifically in case you are hurt or your car is damaged in an accident in which you are at fault. If you are involved in an accident through your own fault you will be subject to an excess (*malus*) which means that your annual premium will be dearer. However, if you avoid any accident, you gain the right to a bonus: your annual premium will be reduced by 5 per cent – which explains the French drivers' obsession with bonuses!

You will also discover the 'amicable statement', (*constat à l'amiable*); you will be given a copy even if you are only going to drive in France for a short holiday. This document must be filled in by both drivers on the spot in the event of a minor accident, then sent to their respective insurance companies. Unless you speak fluent French, do take care to have a *constat* written in English, so as not to put in anything that could subsequently be detrimental to you. Besides, you are not obliged to fill in this report if you do not wish to do so, although that would mean that only the version of the other driver would appear on the report.

Expatriates' check-list

Before leaving Britain:

- Contact the French Consulate for residence permits

- Obtain a change of residence certificate for French Customs

- Get estimates from removal companies

- Make sure that your pets are vaccinated and covered by a health certificate

- Ask your doctor for proof that your children have all the usual vaccinations so that you can register them at a French school

- Make sure that your motoring documents are in order for Customs. Consider buying a new car less than six months before you leave, to avoid paying VAT and road tax in Britain

- Enquire about continuing your insurance policy from abroad

- Contact the DHSS (medical cover, child benefit, pensions, etc.)
- Make your new address known to your bank, building society, credit card companies, insurance companies, solicitor, accountant, the Inland Revenue.

- Make arrangements for payment of recurring liabilities, e.g. rates, mortgage, life insurance, house insurance, etc.

- Consider applying for an international credit card if you do not already have one

- Leave with your solicitor or another trustworthy person a list of instructions in the event of your demise – including funeral arrangements

Last-minute arrangements:

- Get the electricity/gas meters read and ask for a telephone bill

- Cancel club/mail order subscriptions

- Arrange a mail-forwarding service with the Post Office

- If the house is to be left empty, disconnect the main services

On arrival in France:

- Register at the nearest Consulate

- Contact the local Préfecture or Town Hall for your *Carte de Séjour*

- Change your driver's licence, obtain a vehicle licence (*carte grise*), change the number plates, get road tax and car insurance

- If you are a National Insurance pensioner, contact the French social security about obtaining their benefits

- If you are retired, open a bank account so that your pension can be transferred from Britain.

DECLARATION D'IMPORTATION DE MOBILIER
ET D'EFFETS PERSONNELS
(STATEMENT OF IMPORTATION)

Je soussign (1)..

déclare transférer mon domicile de (2)...............................

....

(3)...

et solliciter l'admission en franchise des objets et biens de valeur
repris l'inventaire ci-joint.

Je déclare en outre:

(1) que des biens de valeur, en cours d'usage, m'appartiennent
depuis *Trois* mois ou plus, et sont bien destinés mon utilisation personnelle.

(2) que j'ai pris connaissance des interdictions selon lesquelles les
objects admis en franchise ne peuvent:

(a) être utilisés d'autres usages que ceux pour lesquels la
franchise a ét accordée, sans que soient acquittés les droits et
taxes y afférant

(b) être cédés ou prêtés titre gratuit ou onéreux pendant une
période de *Douze* mois, comptés partir de la date d'enregis-
trement de la déclaration d'importation sans avoir acquitt les
droits en vigueur au moment de la cession ou prêt.

Fait à.................le.......................

(1) Nom et prénoms
(2) Adresse en Grande Bretagne
(3) Adresse en France

Signature:

NB: Mention recopier la fin de l'inventaire
(To be written at the end of the inventory):

'Je déclare que ces objets et biens de valeur en cours d'usage
m'appartiennent depuis plus de *trois* mois et sont bien destinés
mon utilisation personnelle.'

USEFUL ADDRESSES

London

French Consulate General
21 Cromwell Road
Kensington
London SW1 2DQ
01-581 5292

Visas:
College House
29/31 Wright's Lane
London W8
Tel: 01-937 1202

Towns and Counties Under the Jurisdiction of the French ConsulateGeneralinLondon:

Avon	Kent
Bedfordshire	Leicestershire
Berkshire	London
Buckinghamshire	Mid-Glamorgan
Cambridge	Norfolk
Cornwall (inc. Scilly Isles)	Northamptonshire
Devon	Oxfordshire
Dorset	Powis (excl. Montgomery)
Dyfed	Somerset
East Sussex	South Glamorgan
Essex	St Helen's Island
Falkland Islands	Suffolk
Gibraltar	Surrey
Gloucestershire	Warwickshire
Gwent	E/West Glamorgan
Hampshire	West Sussex
Hereford and Worcester	Wiltshire
Hertfordshire	

People residing in other parts of the country must contact the FrenchConsulate nearest to their home:

Liverpool

French Consulate General
523-535 Cunard Building
Pier Head, Liverpool L3 1ET
Tel: 051-236 8685

Edinburgh

French Consulate General
7–11 Randolph Crescent
Edinburgh EH3 7TT
Tel: 031-225 7954/5

Jersey and Guernsey

Northern Ireland

French Consulate
Philip Le Feuvre House
La Motte Street
St Helier, Jersey
Tel: (0534) 26256

Please refer to the French Consulate General in Liverpool.
Andorra Representative
c/o Marie-rose Picart de Francais
63 Westover Road
London SW18 2RS
Tel: 01-874 4086

Ministry of Agriculture,
Fisheries and Food
Animals Health Division 1B
Hook Rise South
Kingston Bybass
Surbiton
Surrey KT6 7NF
Tel: 01-337 6611

Department of Health and Social
Security
Overseas Branch
Newcastle Upon Tyne NE98 1YR
Tel: 091 285 7111

DHSS Child Benefit Centre
PO Box 1
Newcastle Upon Tyne NE88 1AA
Tel: 091 416 6722

HM Customs and Excise
King's Beam House
Mark Lane
London EC3R 7HE
Tel: 01-626 1515

The Expatriates' Association
PO Box 24
Warminster
Wiltshire BA12 9YL
Tel: 0985 212236

In France

Centre de Renseignements
Douaniers
19 Rue St Homore
75001 Paris
Tel: 42 60 35 90

Ministère des Affaires Sociales,
de la Sant et de la Famille
8 Avenue de Ségur
75007 Paris
Tel: 45 67 55 44

Fédération Française des Sociétés
d'Assurances (FFSA)
26 Boulevard Haussmann
75009 Paris
Tel: 42 47 90 00
(For names of insurance
companies)

Bureau Régional d'Industrialisa-
tion et d'Accueil MIDI-
PYRENEES-BRIA-
14 Rue de Tivoli
(Grand – Rond)
31000 Toulouse
Tel: 61 33 50 97
(For information and documenta-
tion in English on settling in the
South-West)

Préfecture de Police
7 Boulevard du Palais
75004 Paris
Tel: 42 60 33 22
       42 29 21 55

Social Security Information
Services
69 bis Rue de Dunkergle
75453 Paris Cedex 09
Tel: 42 80 63 67
(Minitel: 3615 + SECSOC)

11
FAMILY LIFE

THE EDUCATION SYSTEM

In France, every child from 6 to 16 must, by law, attend school. You can choose between two types of school:

- state schools, called 'public' schools (not to be confused with British public schools, which are quite the opposite); these are free and secular. However, books and stationery are paid for by parents.
- private schools; these are fee paying and often religious. The rates are not astronomical, as most of these schools get state aid.

Nursery Schools

Children start school at six and not at five as in Britain; the vast majority go to nursery school from the age of three (or even two, if they are toilet-trained). The French are proud of their nursery schools and rightly so, as they are considered to be amongst the best in the world. (You even have bilingual nursery schools.) Even at this level there is a choice between public and private kinder-gartens, the latter being fee paying. It is not compulsory to send your children to nursery school, but most French people do because it's an excellent preparation for primary school.

Nursery schools are divided into three sections: in the 'small' and 'middle' sections (two to four years and four to five years) they are taught personal hygiene and creative activities; in the 'big' section (five to six years) they begin to learn reading, writing and maths, drawing, painting and pottery.

Beyond nursery school, all educational establishments, whether state or private, follow the same syllabus and have the same structure.

Primary Schools

These are divided into three sections: lower school, middle school and upper school.

Lower School (cycle préparatoire)
This is also known as the 11th class since, in the French school system, they do not count the number of classes from 1 to 12 but backwards from 11 to the final year, the culmination of which is the end-of-year examination, the *baccalauréat*.

This *cycle préparatoire* lasts one year.

Middle School
This lasts for two years (CE1 and CE2 or 10th and 9th classes) and is known as the *cycle élémentaire*.

Upper School (cycle moyen)
This lasts two years (CM1 and CM2) or 8th and 7th classes.

Secondary Education

Children will attend a C.E.S. (*Collège d'enseignement secondaire*) then a *Lycée* or else go straight to a *Lycée*. It will depend on local facilities, the childrens' aptitude, their future studies, etc. In as much as such comparisons are possible, the 'College' is somewhat like a comprehensive, the *Lycée* more like a secondary or grammar school. In the *Collèges*, classes go from 6th to 3rd (that is three years before the end of secondary schooling). At the end of the 3rd class, at the age of about 15, pupils can take a *Brevet des Collèges* (secondary schools examination). This allows pupils to proceed to competitive examinations (*concours*) for recruitment into some branches of the Public Service, and replaces the entrance examination for some specialist training schools. NB: A pupil who fails the *Brevet* is not excluded from going onto further education.

At the end of the 3rd class, according to their personal abilities, the advice of their teachers and the wishes of their parents, pupils work either towards the *Baccalauréat*, or a technical diploma (*Brevet de Technicien*), a vocational diploma (*Brevet d'Etudes Professionnelles*) or a vocational training certificate (*Certificat d'Aptitude Professionnelle*).

All these choices are explained in a leaflet available from the French Ministry of Education, entitled 'After the 3rd Class' (*Après la Classe d·· 3ème*).

The *Lycées* prepare pupils for the *Baccalauréat* in either general or technical education. Private schools also work towards the same goal.

There are two important points about the *Baccalauréat*. Firstly, it is divided into several sections – literary, scientific, mathematical, languages etc – where the accent, in each case, is on the discipline concerned. Pupils are directed towards, or choose, a section according to their abilities or the university studies or business career they wish to pursue. The second point is that within each section they must take exams in all subjects without exception; they cannot choose only their favourite subjects. Within each section, the *Baccalauréat* exam is the same throughout France. Here too the Ministry of Education can provide a whole range of documents and brochures on the options open to your child.

Further Education

After the *Baccalauréat*, students have a choice between two types of further education:

1. A so-called 'vocational' system, (*système d'orientation*) for which they only need to have passed the *Baccalauréat* in their specialized section to get into university. This applies to law, management and economic sciences, fine arts, social sciences, science, medicine, dentistry and pharmacy. Selection takes place during the course.

2. A so-called 'selection' system, (*système de sélection*) which requires the *Baccalauréat* plus a competitive examination, or the *Baccalauréat* plus a school record and an appearance before an examining board. This system is in force:

- in University Institutes of Technology (IUT) within universities
- in Institutes of Political Studies (IEP)
- in 'post-baccalauréat' establishments which prepare for the Advanced Technical Diploma (*Brevet de Technicien Supérieur – BTS*) and train para-medics

- in the university academies (*grandes écoles*): National Administration School, (*Ecole Nationale d'Administration or E.N.A.*) Higher Teacher Training College, (*Ecole Normale Supérieure*) Further Commercial Education, (*Hautes Etudes Commerciales or H.E.C.*), Polytechnic etc. These schools are the cream of the French education system. They are geared towards specific, high-powered careers. For example, the E.N.A. is a passport to top civil service, the *Normale Supérieure* to top teaching posts and so on. The selection procedures are rigorous but young people who come out are sure not only of a job but of a possibly brilliant career.

In general, you should contact your child's school to arrange a meeting with the careers officer and obtain any documents likely to be of interest. Parents' associations are also in a position to give you information and useful addresses.

Parents' Associations

They play a very important role in school life. The Parents' Association is represented at school boards, who vote on budgeting, the internal management of the college or school, and give opinions and put forward suggestions to the head teacher on the educational running of the school and extra curricular activities. It is also present at parents–teachers meetings, which are more directly concerned with the problems and activities of each class within the school.

In comparison with the anglo-saxon countries, French education tends to demand a lot from its children on an intellectual level. There is often much homework, lengthening the youngsters' schoolday by several hours' work at home. Sport, for a long time the poor relation in the French system, is now much more widespread. Sports centres are springing up all over the country and they are usually very well equipped. (If you ever pass through Vichy, the multi-sports centre 'Pierre Coulon', on the banks of the River Allier is well worth a visit.)

Settling In For Foreign Children

It is not always easy for a child who does not speak fluent French to adapt to the school system after the ages of eight or nine, especially in a state school and even more so in a town. In the country, where classes are smaller, your child will have a better chance of perfecting his or her French before having to concentrate on studies.

Alternatively there are bilingual schools where lessons are taught in French and English at the same time; many young foreigners go to these schools. In the event of there not being one near your home, you may benefit from finding a private school where classes are not too big and where your children will receive special attention which will help them to learn French well. You can then decide whether or not they should be integrated into a state school.

The *Baccalauréat* includes an international option, which is offered in some schools. Certain subjects are taught in two languages: French and the language of the chosen option (English or American, Spanish, Italian etc.). The teaching of language and literature is complemented by history and geography, also in both tongues. French and foreign students who are bilingual and are thus capable of following both a general education in French and specific teaching in the language of the option can be enrolled in these international classes.

If you have any problems or questions concerning the education of your children in France, do not hesitate to contact the Parents' Association (APEL) at the Lycée Français Charles de Gaulle in London before you leave (the address is at the end of the chapter). APEL will be able to give you the information you require, in English, as well as the benefit of their vast personal experience of bilingual education.

The French attach very great importance to the education of their children, whatever their social background. For generations, education has been considered the best springboard to career and social success – although the anglo-saxon ethic that favours a spirit of initiative and a business sense is beginning to make serious inroads into this mentality. In spite of everything, education remains the one subject capable of bringing people out onto the streets, whether parents, teachers, students or schoolchildren, if they think that the authorities are interfering with some aspect of the system. The problem is that all education ministers do, in fact, feel obliged to promote reforms, whether good or bad, to make their mark in a very important and vote-catching area. Obviously, when they get it wrong, the backlash is painful...

Because the French educational system is one and the same right across the country, and has been since the time of Napoleon, reforms can be implemented quite easily. Napoleon's dream was that in all schools, in all of France, children in the same level class would be studying the same lesson at the same time. This strict military objective has happily never been achieved; French schools are however, all subject to the same syllabus and the same examinations. They also remain subject to quite rigid disciplinary rules which some people find very formal: corporal punishment is forbidden but unexplained absences, the forging of parents' signatures, or hooliganism rapidly lead to expulsion.

NB: If you send your children to a state school, you should know that since the law of 1959, you must send them to the school nearest to your house. You can ask the *Mairie* in the area where you are going to live for a list of local schools. If you have a preference for a particular school you would do well to choose a house located in the catchment area of that school.

MARRIAGE

Civil marriages only are legal in France. Religious ceremonies for those who want them, must take place after the civil wedding. The minister, priest or rabbi will inform you about the formalities pertaining to the religious service.

For the civil marriage, the steps to take are as follows:

1. You must publish the banns, that is the public declaration of the marriage, at the town hall (*la Mairie*) of the district in which one of the couple lives or where he or she has been living for at least one month. A foreigner must show his residence permit as proof of residence.

2. In order for the banns to be published, you must supply the council offices with:

- **Birth certificates** of the future married couple. For a foreigner this document must be stamped by the local consulate of his native country.
- **Medical certificates** issued by a French doctor not later than two months before approaching the *Mairie*. Pre-marital medical checks have been compulsory in France for a long

time and were designed to check incompatibility between the blood groups of the couple, which might have caused problems for their children (particularly the rhesus factor). Today, with AIDS spreading, these examinations have taken on a new importance. Nevertheless, the results are strictly confidential and cannot, in themselves, stop the wedding.

- If you are divorced, you must produce a **divorce certificate**; if you are a widow or widower, the **death certificate** of your spouse. Either document must be translated into French and validated by your consulate.

A widow must wait 300 days after the death of her husband before she can re-marry; the same period of waiting (300 days of separate residence from her ex-spouse) is imposed on a woman divorcee. Alternatively, the woman must produce medical evidence that she is not pregnant. Any child born during this time is considered to be the issue of the former husband. Where divorce is concerned, this kind of detail is important!

3. If you and your spouse are both of British nationality and registered with the British Consulate, you would be wise to file a copy of your marriage certificate with the consulate. If, later on, once you have returned to Britain, you decide to divorce, the British authorities will need to know about and recognize your marriage.

The marriage takes place at the *Mairie*, in the presence of at least two witnesses, one for each of the couple. It is possible to have two each but no more. The Mayor or one of his deputies officiates. The service is free. Copies of the marriage certificate can only be obtained at the *Mairie*. You will also be given a 'Family Booklet' (*Livret de Famille*) in which you are required by law to note all the official events which concern your family life: birth of each child, eventual deaths, divorce etc.

The age of consent for marriage in France is 18. Up till then the consent of at least one parent is required, (or grand-parent if the parents are dead). If this consent is refused, there is no legal recourse at all.

In France, marriage is subject to a special 'system' (*régime*), which governs the way in which assets are shared or divided. If you marry without a contract, you are automatically subject to the system of 'common acquired assets' (*Communaut des Biens Réduite aux Acquets*): this means that any assets bought during the marriage belong to both husband and wife; any asset bought beforehand or obtained through inheritance (even during the marriage) remains the private property of each individual. Another system or *régime* often applied is the 'system of separate assets' (*Régime de la Séparation des Biens*). This requires a contract, drawn up by a notary.

If you have any assets in the UK and you marry in France, you would be wise to consult a lawyer to find out what could be the effect of the marriage on your properties. If these assets belonged to you before your marriage, there is no problem, but if you and your spouse buy a house in Britain after the wedding, everything will depend on what 'system' you were married under if there is a final shareout in the event of a divorce. If you have removable objects, like furniture, pictures, etc. they will be considered common assets unless there is proof to the contrary.

BIRTH

A child born in France of foreign parents is only given French nationality if the country of origin of his parents does not automatically grant him the same nationality as them. A child born of British parents therefore will be British. However, if one of the parents is French by nationality or birth, the child will be French, unless he gives up this nationality in the six months preceding his 18th birthday.

If he retains his French nationality, a boy will have to do military service even if he does not live in France. Not being aware of this detail has sometimes caused trouble for young men who have come to spend their holidays in France after their 18th birthday and have found themselves liable to a prison sentence for desertion!

Registration

A birth must be registered within three working days at the *Mairie* of the place of birth, on presentation of a birth certificate signed by the obstetrician or midwife. It is also important to register the birth at the British Consulate, so that the child will be eligible for a British passport.

Adoption

If you want to adopt a child, your foreign nationality will not be a problem. You will be treated just like French citizens. If you already have adopted children when you settle in France, make sure that you bring with you the court order authorizing the adoption as well as the birth certificate, just in case you need to prove your status as adoptive parents, for one reason or another.

DIVORCE

The French courts can only judge an action for divorce if one of the two parties is French or if both are residents in France.

Mutual Consent

The quickest divorce is called the 'divorce by mutual consent' (*divorce par consentement mutuel*). You must have been married for at least six months. If both parties are in agreement over the divorce, and over financial, material and family arrangements (custody of children etc.), there is no need to divulge the reasons for divorce. The divorce is granted by a judge without going before a magistrate's court, three months after the application if both parties are still in agreement.

Contested Divorce

In cases where there is disagreement and where one of the couple considers that there are serious causes for divorce (physical or mental cruelty, alcoholism etc.), the case is taken before the courts as in Britain.

Whatever the type of divorce, the services of a lawyer are compulsory. In the case of divorce by mutual consent, the two parties can use the services of the same lawyer. The partition of assets is done in accordance with the 'matrimonial system (régime).

Children

If children are involved, it would be wise to think very carefully about the problems that could arise if you were to take them to Britain. If they are under the jurisdiction of the French courts, you would at least need to obtain the courts' permission. Litigation between parents of two nationalities, arguing about the custody of their children, is unfortunately frequent and always very painful.

DEATH

A death must be registered within 24 hours at the *Mairie* in your neighbourhood or area. A death certificate signed by a doctor registered with the local authority is required, and if the deceased was foreign, his or her long stay residence permit (*carte de séjour*); the family record book (*livret de famille*) is needed for a French national.

Only the *Mairie* can give authorization to close the coffin, at the earliest 24 hours and at the latest six days after the death. It also takes care of the funeral, under the auspices of a funeral director (*Les Pompes Funèbres*). The latter is responsible for all the formalities. You also approach the funeral director if you wish to have the remains or ashes of the deceased sent to Britain. You can also advise the nearest British Consul. If you want the deceased buried in France the Consul will give you the address of a Protestant church or a synagogue (if you do not have it already). If the deceased was a Catholic, all you have to do is contact the parish priest.

Cremation

Cremation is less common in France than in Britain but is on the increase. There must be a request bearing the signature of the deceased or of the person dealing with the ceremonies.

Wills and Inheritance

In France, the existence of a will does not deprive the immediate family of certain specific rights of inheritance, as far as any assets under French legal jurisdiction are concerned. Children will have the right to part of the estate which varies according to their number; the surviving spouse also has the right to part of the estate depending on the number of children. It can be total ownership or a lifelong interest (*usufruit*).

Nevertheless a will can be essential, if you do not want all your property in France to be divided into small parts; a will leaving the house – or its tenure – to the surviving spouse may be necessary.

As stated in Chapter 6, if your tax address is not in France, French law only applies to those properties located in France. If you *are* living in France, your British assets are subject to French law except for real estate. In general, the French authorities will make sure that the will is executed according to the laws of the country where the deceased was fiscally domiciled.

You can make your own will, handwritten, signed and dated by yourself without a witness being present. This is called a holographic testament (from the Greek 'written by hand'). This will is perfectly valid; however, only a lawyer can advise you on the type of will best suited to your own personal circumstances.

If the deceased has assets abroad it is possible that at the time of dividing up the estate, the notary will ask for a certificate of customs (*un certificat de coûtume*). This is a document explaining the heritage laws of the country where the assets are situated. For example, if the deceased owned a Swiss chalet, and death occurred outside Switzerland, the notary or court (in the case of litigation) could ask for a certificate of customs to see who, according to Swiss law, would inherit the chalet.

A final word on the executors of a will: in France, they have no rights to succession of the deceased. They are only there to check that all goes well between the various legatees.

In short...

- For information concerning your children's schooling in France, contact the Parents' Association at the French *Lycée* in London

- State schools are free, but you must pay for books and stationery

- Your child must go to the state school that is in your catchment area; therefore be careful where you decide to live, especially if you have a particular school in mind

- There are bilingual schools in France

- If you get married in France and are both British nationals, get your marriage recognized by British authorities through your nearest Consulate

- If you marry a French national, under the French system, you will be asked under what *régime* you wish to be married, when it comes to properties and belongings. Make sure you marry under the *régime* most appropriate to your circumstances

- In France, a testamentary executor is not entitled to any of the estate

USEFUL ADDRESSES

Education

Bureau de l'Information et de
l'Orientation du Ministère de
l'Education Nationale
61-65 Rue Dutot
75015 Paris

Ministère de l'Education
Nationale
110 Rue de Grenelle
75007 Paris
Tel: 45 50 10 10

Office National d'Information
sur les Enseignements et les
Professions (ONISEP)
46-52 Rue Albert
75013 Paris
Tel: 45 83 32 21

Centre National d'Enseignement
par Correspondance (CNEC)
60 Boulevard du Lycée
92171 Vanves

Centre National de
Documentationsur
l'Enseig ement Privé
20 Rue Fabert
75007 Paris
Tel: 47 05 32 68
(For information on private and
bilingual schools)

Service d'Information des
Familles
277 Rue Saint Jacques
75005 Paris
For information on British,
bilingual or international schools
in France:
AAWE Guide to Education in
France
27 Rue Lhomond
75005 Paris

British Institute
11 Rue Constantine
75007 Paris
Tel: 45 55 95 95

British Council
11 Rue Constantine
75007 Paris
Tel: 45 55 95 95

British Consulate in Paris
16 Rue d'Anjou
75008 Paris
Tel: 42 66 91 42

British Consulate–General in
Lille
11 Square Dutilleul
59800 Lille
Tel: 20 57 87 90

British Consulate–General in
Bordeaux
15 Cours de Verdun
33081 Bordeaux
Tel: 56 52 28 35

British Consulate–General in
Lyon
24 Rue Childebert
69288 Lyon
Tel: 78 37 59 67

British Consulate–General in Marseilles
24 Avenue du Prado
13006 Marseille
Tel: 91 53 43 32

British & Commonwealth Women's Association
7 Rue Auguste Vacquerie
75016 Paris
Tel: 47 20 01 36

In London:

Lycée Français Charles de Gaulle
35 Cromwell Road
London SW7 2DG
Tel: 01-584 6322

Some Churches

Church of England

St George's Church
7 Rue Auguste Vacquerie
75016 Paris
Tel: 47 20 22 51

St Nicholas's Church
10 Cours Xavier-Arnozan
Bordeaux
Tel: 56 06 37 17

All Saints Church
Rue de Belloi
Marseilles
Tel: 42 22 48 71

Wesleyon Methodist Church
4 Rue Roguépihe
75008 Paris

St Michael's Church
5 Rue d'Aguesseau
75008 Paris
Tel: 47 42 70 88

Les Mains Ouvertes
La Part-Dieu
Lyons
Tel: 78 59 67 06

Church of Scotland
17 Rue Bayard
75008 Paris
Tel: 47 20 90 49

Jewish

Consistoire Israélite de Paris
44 Rue de la Victoire
75009 Paris
Tel: 45 26 90 15
(For information on location of
synagogues)

Catholic

St Joseph's Church
50 Avenue Hoche
75008 Paris
Tel: 42 27 28 56

GLOSSARY

A

Achat en viager: To buy against an annuity payable to the beneficiary throughout his lifetime.

Accusé de réception: Acknowledgment of receipt of letter/package to sender.

Apport personnel: Cash-deposit.

Arrhes: Sum of money which one person hands over to another at the point of concluding a contract to ensure its enforcement.

Agent immobilier: Estate agent.

Allocations familiales: Child allowances.

Allocations pré ou post natales: Maternity benefits.

B

Bail: Lease contract by which a property is let for a fixed term and price.

Bans de mariage: Banns – announcement of marriage published at the town hall.

C

Constat: Spoken or written statement officially recognising or describing a situation (e.g. accident, break-in, etc).

Carnet de santé: Document given to a mother on the birth of a child, on which the medical history of the child is recorded.

Coproprieté: Co-ownership – situation of people who share the ownership of a property (block of flats, houses on an estate etc).

Charges d'un appartement: Service charges – sums payable by the tenant in addition to rent, or by the co-owners for sundry taxes and daily upkeep of the block of flats.

Contrat synallagmatique: Contract whereby both parties are equally bound to each other, (e.g. a sale).

Certificat d'urbanisme: Certificate from the housing authorities in towns.

Constructeur: Builder.

Caution: Deposit of guarantee.

Compromis de vente: A simple contract signifying the agreement of both parties on a sale before the notary is involved.

D

Droits de préemption: Official right of precedence of one purchaser over another, at the same price.

Dessous de table: Sum paid secretly and illegally to the vendor by a purchaser in a transaction, in addition to the declared sum.

Droit de passage: Right of way – right to pass through the property of another person (right of way is legal in the case of a enclave, and contractual in other cases).

Déduction: Sum subtracted from the amount of income to be declared, e.g.: energy savings, charities.

Double vitrage: Double glazing.

Domicile principal: Residence which is occupied at least 8 months out of 12.

Domicile fiscal: Home or place of residence which is also the centre of economic interests.

Devis: Estimate.

E

Ecole maternelle: Nursery school.

Ecole privée: Fee-paying school.

Ecole publique: State school.

Etat des lieux: Inventory of fixtures – document drawn up between the owner and tenant of a house or flat setting out the condition of the property when the tenants move in and when they move out.

Entrepreneur: Contractor. (In French this word has a completely different meaning from the word 'entrepreneur' as used in Britain.) It means a person or company who carries out building or public works.

F

Fermage: Rent of a farm or arable land. Dues paid to the owner by the farmer.

Fosse septique: Septic tank – installation destined for the sterilization of waste matter from houses.

Fonds de commerce: Stock (in trade), business (as opposed to commercial *property*).

Forfait (prix à forfait): Lump sum.

G

Gérant d'immeubles: Manager of a block of flats. The person who manages and professionally administers blocks of flats belonging to other people. Today the manager is often a company rather than an individual person.

Geomètre: Technician who works out in an appropriate way, the dimensions or surface area of landed property and defines the limits of it.

Gérant: Independent manager.

H

Huissier: Bailiff – among other things can be responsible for affidavits.

Hypothèque: Mortgage – right given to a creditor on a property belonging to a debtor. The debtor does not lose the mortgaged property but he cannot dispose of it freely. In the case of the debtor not being able to pay his mortgage, the creditor has priority and may have the property sold in order to recover the money owed to him.

I

Incinérer: To cremate.

L

Lettre recommandée: Registered letter.
Livret de famille: Document given to a couple when they are married, by the mayor, in which must be noted any changes in their civil status, such as the birth of children.

M

Mandat: Power of attorney; proxy.
Mairie: Town hall; council offices (in small town or village).
Maire: Mayor.
Mutuelle: Private insurance – members are insured against certain risks or are given certain social or medical benefits against payment of contributions.
Mitoyenneté: Common ownership – co-ownership of a wall, a fence separating two properties, two blocks of flats, certified by a notary.

O

Ordre des Avocats: Association grouping the members of a profession (lawyers...) and administered by a council of members. The same thing occurs in *L'Ordre des Architectes, L'Ordre des Geomètres-Experts*, etc.

P

Patrimoine: Personal estate; heritage.
Permis de résident: Resident's permit.
Plus value: Capital Gains Tax.
Pompes funèbres: Undertakers.

Préavis: Advance notice – notice which must be observed before breaking a contract, or an agreement.

Promoteur immobilier: Property developer.

Q

Quote-part: Individual, proportional share in a contribution or an acquisition.

Quotient familial: Family quota – obtained by dividing the taxable income of a specific person into a number of parts, (i.e. members of a family) with a view to reducing income tax.

R

Retraité: Pensioner.

S

Syndic: Person (or company) responsible for representing the common interests of a legally formed group of people.

Saisie: Foreclosure – a court order where a debtor's property is held to force him to carry out his obligations.

Sous-Seing (Acte Sous-Seing): Signing of a deed not registered with a notary (pre-contract of sale).

Servitude: Legal obligations applied to a property for the profit of another property belonging to a different owner.

T

TVA: VAT.

Tiers provisionnels: Three-part payments of income tax, representing one third each of the amount owed for the current year.

Tacite reconduction: Tacit renewal of a lease, the tenant continuing to use the premises without opposition from the leaseholder.

Tout-à-l'égout: Mains sewers. System which evacuates sewage from a house straight into the town's sewers.

Testament: Will.

Testament olographe: Holographic will – one written out by hand in full, dated and signed by the testator.

Travailleur indépendant: Self-employed person.

V

Viabilité: General basic work to be carried out on a site before any building is done, e.g. roads, water, gas, electricity, sewers, telephone.

Vignette: Road tax.

BIBLIOGRAPHY

IN ENGLISH

Living in France Today, Philip Holland. Hale.

Michelin Green Guides on various regions of France.

Documents provided by the French Industrial Development Board and by the Department of Trade and Industry on Business in France.

Documents provided by the DHSS in Britain.

Employment Abroad – A Guide to the Tax Problems
David Ross, The Institute of Chartered Accountants.

Resident Abroad Magazine, 102–108 Clerkenwell Road, London EC1. Tel: 01–251 9321

*Homes Overseas, 387 City Road, London EC1V 1NA
Tel: 01-278 9232*

IN FRENCH

General Information on the Regions

Editions Christine Bonneton – Collection Encyclopédies Régionales: Alsace, Berry, Bourbonnais, Champagne, Corse, Dauphiné, Franche-Comté, Limousin, Lorraine, Normandie, Pays du Nord, Picardie, Poitou, Savoie, Touraine-Orléanais.

Information on Architecture

L'Architecture Rurale et Bourgeoise en France. Georges Doyon and Robert Hubrecht, (Editions Ch. Massin et Cie).

Information on Buying, Restoring and Building

Comment Acheter, Louer, Améliorer Votre Logement, Jean-Pierre Bourbonnais, (Editions du Moniteur).

Appartement, Maison: Comment Bien Acheter et Bien l'Aménager, Daniel Puiboube, (Guide Marabout).

Construire une Maison – Conseils d'un Architecte, Bernard Jeannel, (Editions du Moniteur).

Free booklets:

Vous et le Notaire
Vous et le Constructeur
Vous et l'Agent Immobilier
Vous et le Syndic de Copropriété
Vous et l'Architecte

Ministère de l'Urbanisme et du Logement

Free booklet:

Vous Achetez un Logement: Quels Sont Vos Droits?

On financial possibilities:

Le Crédit Immobilier – Savoir Choisir, (Editions Nathan/Banque La Hénin).

Magazines on Properties to Buy or Rent

On sale at newsagents:

Indicateur Bertrand

Locations-Ventes
De Particulier Particulier
La Centrale des Particuliers
Catalogue Lagrange

Free from estate agents:

Partout published by 'Les Agences Françaises'. Contains not only house ads, but also commercial properties.

Bookshops:
The European Bookshop, 4 Regent Place, London W1R 6BH.
Tel: 01-734 5259.

MORE USEFUL ADDRESSES

Information Centres on accommodation Outside Paris (known as Associations Départementales pour l'Information Logement – ADIL)

Ain
34 Rue du Général-Delestraint
01011 Bourg-en-Bresse
Tel: 74 21 95 00

Allier
35 Bis Rue de Bellecroix
03402 Yzeure
Tel: 70 44 41 57

28 Rue Paul Constans
031000 Montluçon
Tel: 70 28 42 04

2 Boulevard de Russie
03200 Vichy
Tel: 70 98 18 45

Alpes de Haute Provence
42 Boulevard Victor-Hugo
04004 Digne
Tel: 92 31 57 29

Alpes Maritimes
10 Rue de Paris
06000 Nice
Tel: 93 85 92 48

6 Rue Forville
06400 Cannes
Tel: 93 39 38 00

Ardennes
38 Bd Georges Poirier
08002 Charleville-Mezières
Tel: 24 58 28 92

Aube
Hôtel du Départment
10026 Troyes
Tel: 25 42 50 50

Côte d'Or
Hôtel du Départment
21035 Dijon
Tel: 80 74 02 37

Dordogne
5 Rue Victor Hugo
24000 Périgueux
Tel: 53 53 44 35

Gard
1 Place Duguesclin
30000 Nîmes
Tel: 66 21 22 23

Gironde
11 Cours du Chapeau Rouge
33000 Bordeaux
Tel: 56 48 00 52

Jura
16 Rue des Cordeliers
39000 Lons le Saunier
Tel: 84 24 68 38

Loire Atlantique
6 Rue de l'Arche Sèche
44000 Nantes
Tel: 40 89 30 15

Lot
51 Rue de Brives
46000 Cahors
Tel: 65 35 25 41

Meurthe et Moselle
Place des Ducs de Bar
54000 Nancy
Tel: 83 27 62 72

Côtes du Nord
1 Rue Chateaubriand
22011 Saint-Brieuc
Tel: 96 61 66 70

Drôme
31 Rue Faventines
26000 Valence
Tel: 75 43 74 01

Haute Garonne
3 Rue St Antoihe
31000 Toulouse
Tel: 61 22 46 22

Indre
23 Rue Mousseaux
36000 Châteauroux
Tel: 54 27 37 37

Centre d'Information sur
l'Habitat
8 Rue d'Anjou
44600 Saint Nazaire
Tel: 40 66 80 29

Mayenne
10 Rue de Strasbourg
53006 Laval
Tel: 43 53 13 66

Morbihan
2 C Boulevard Franchet
d'Esperey
56100 Lorient
Tel: 97 21 74 64

Nord

1 Rue de Beaumont
59140 Dunkerque
Tel: 28 63 23 40

1 Place Porte Notre Dame
59400 Cambrai
Tel: 27 81 15 83

Centre d'Information sur
l'habitat
44/45 Place Victor
Hassenbroucq
59200 Tourcoing
Tel: 20 24 92 04

64 Rue Canteleu
59599 Douai
Tel: 27 97 36 27

Hôtel de Ville
17 Grand'Place
59100 Roubaix
Tel: 20 73 62 62

12 Avenue d'Amsterdam
59300 Valenciennes
Tel: 27 42 67 87

Puy de Dôme

Résidence du Parc
38 Av. Vercingétorix
63000 Clermont Ferrand
Tel: 73 93 76 96

Hautes Pyrénées

Résidence Brasilia
24 Rue Larrey
65000 Tarbes
Tel: 62 34 67 11

Haute Saône

26 Rue de Fleurier
70000 Vesoul
Tel: 84 75 60 19

Saône et Loire

13 Rue Gabriel Jeanton
71000 Mâcon
Tel: 85 39 30 70

24 Rue Sainte Barbe
71200 Le Creusot
Tel: 85 56 01 10

11 Rue du Pont
71100 Chalon sur Saône
Tel: 85 48 76 88

Place du Champ de Foire
71600 Paray le Monial
Tel: 85 81 04 20

Haute Savoie

4 Avenue de Chambéry
74000 Annecy
Tel: 50 45 79 72

Paris

Centre Information dogement
2 Rue des Capulines
7500? Paris
Tel: 45 49 14 14

204 Rue Lecourbe
75015 Paris
Tel: (1) 45 31 14 50

Seine Maritime

Pont Rue Tous Vents
76100 Rouen Saint Sever
Tel: 35 72 58 50

8 Rue de l'Oranger
76200 Dieppe
Tel: 35 04 94 17

87 Rue Richelieu
76600 Le Havre
Tel: 35 43 71 61

Seine et Marne

Federation du Logement
42A Resido Chenonceax
77100 Meaux
Tel: 60 25 14 43

1 Rue Jacques Amyot
77000 Melun
Tel: (1) 64 52 46 63

3 Place de l'Arche-Guédon
77200 Torcy
Tel: 60 05 72 72

Tarn et Garonne

2 Quai de Verdun
82000 Montauban
Tel: 63 63 04 68

Var

44 Rue Picot
83000 Toulon
Tel: 94 93 46 02

1 Boulevard Foch
83007 Draguignan
Tel: 94 67 35 44

Vaucluse

4 Bis Place Jérusalem
84000 Avignon
Tel: 90 85 84 10

Vienne
16 Bis Rue Boncenne
86000 Poitiers
Tel: 49 88 31 93

94 Boulevard Blossac
86100 Châtellerault
Tel: 49 23 50 24 (p.m. only)

Yonne
58 Bd Vauban
89000 Auxerre
Tel: 86 52 64 56

Val D'Oise
Les Oréades
Parvis de la Préfecture
95000 Cergy
Tel: (1) 30 32 14 22

7 Rue Christino Garcia
Tour Europe
95600 Eaubonne
Tel: (1) 39 59 33 77

47 Ave Paul Vacéry
95200 Sarcelles
Tel: (1) 34 19 32 09